QUILTER'S PRECISE YARDAGE GUIDE

QUILTER'S PRECISE YARDAGE GUIDE

Carol Ann Waugh and Judith LaBelle

New Century Publishers, Inc.

Printing Code
11   12   13   14   15   16

Library of Congress Cataloging in Publication Data

Waugh, Carol.
  Quilters precise yardage guide.

  1. Quilting. I. LaBelle, Judith. II. Title.
TT835.W38 1983   746.9′7   82-24622
ISBN   0-8329-0275-6

Cover Photograph by Patricia Rothkow.

Contents

Acknowledgment

Special thanks to Anthony J. Capato—a programmer and a friend—who wrote the basic programs for the generation of the yardage charts for our *Patchworking* book and modified these programs so this new book could be generated totally by using a microcomputer. Without his assistance, this book would never have been written since by our "manual" calculations, figuring out these charts would have taken a total of 178,320 separate calculations. We figured out that if we completed 6 calculations per minute, working 4 hours a day, it would have taken us 124 days just to complete the charts. And that's without double checking the accuracy of the results—or typing the charts. Considering that both of us also like to make quilts, the sacrifice of writing this book without the help of a computer would have been too much! So, thanks to Tony, we were able to generate this book and still have plenty of time to create new quilt designs and get on with the fun of quilt making.

Introduction

Making a quilt can be an exhilarating experience—whether you are making a quilt which is your own unique design or one which was inspired by a quilt which you saw in a book or at a quilt exhibit. Either way, to translate your design into a reality, you must answer the following questions:

What templates do I need to make?
How much fabric do I need to buy?

Many books on quilt making are frustrating to use for they assume that the reader knows the answers to these questions.

In our previous books, *The Patchwork Quilt Design & Coloring Book* and *Patchworking*, we provided detailed instructions on how to determine what templates you need and the necessary yardage to buy. But these instructions only covered the quilt designs included in our books. The response to our techniques was strong, enthusiastic, and our readers requested more.

So because yardage calculation is a tedious and time-consuming task, we decided to compile a comprehensive yardage chart book which will enable quilt makers who are using square, rectangular or triangular templates to easily look up the required yardage for templates ranging in size from as small as 1 inch to as large as 25 inches, in ½-inch increments.

All the charts in this book were generated from an Atari home computer program which was written for us by Anthony J. Capato. Using this program, you can determine the yardage requirements for square, rectangular or triangular templates of any size. If you have an Atari computer with a disk drive and would like to have a copy of this program, simply send a check for $15.00 to Dekotek, Inc, P.O. Box 1863, Grand Central Station, New York, NY 10017.

QUILTER'S PRECISE YARDAGE GUIDE

Chapter 1

How To Use This Book

Before using the yardage charts, you must draw a grid of your quilt design, determine the number and size of each template and the number of times that it is used in the design, and look up the template code for that template, as explained below.

Drawing the Grid

Once you have decided on the quilt design you will use, draw the design on a grid which represents the entire quilt top. Since this grid will serve as the basis for determining the size of each template, this grid must be drawn to scale with great precision. We suggest using pre-printed graph paper. Choose the size of the graph paper in relation to the type of design you are using. For example, the more complex the design, the smaller the squares on the graph paper. Three-patch designs will work best using three or six squares to the inch graph paper, four-patch designs will work best on graph paper measuring four or eight squares to the inch, and so forth.

Determining the Template Size

Once you have drawn your grid and colored it to indicate the different fabrics you will use and the placement of each, determine the overall measurements of your quilt top. Since the grid represents the entire top, each square of the grid represents a certain portion of the quilt top. For example, if the quilt top is to be 60″ × 80″ and you are using graph paper measuring four squares to the inch, you would lay out the quilt top grid with 6 inches across and 8 inches down. Each of the inches would represent 10″ in reality. Each little square in the inch would represent 2½ inches.

To illustrate this, we have created a new design which we call "The Daily Star," which is shown below. We have also drawn a grid which indicates how this block would fit in the overall quilt top—The Daily Star would be repeated in each of the blocks outlined.

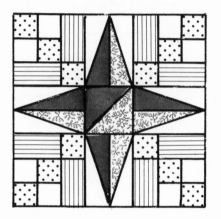

Since we know that each small square in the grid represents 2½ inches, we can easily determine that the templates needed to create this design would be of the sizes indicated below:

Square 2½″ × 2½″

Rectangle 2½″ × 5″

Triangle (based on square) 2½″ × 2½″

Triangle (based on rectangle) 2½″ × 5″

Determining the Template Code

Referring to Chapter 4, you will find a list of the square templates included in the book. Simply look up the measurement 2½″ × 2½″ and you will find that the template code is S4. Look up the code for the rectangle in Chapter 6 and triangles in Chapters 5 and 7. (Note that we have two sections of charts for triangles. The first, in Chapter 5, includes triangles with two equal sides. These triangles have codes beginning with "TR", and since they may be created by dividing a square in half diagonally, will most often be found in designs composed mostly of squares. For example, triangle TR15 will work in combination with square S15. The second section, in Chapter 7, includes triangles which have unequal sides. These triangles, which have codes beginning with "T", may be created by dividing a rectangle in half diagonally and the template sizes given correspond to the sizes of the rectangular templates. For example, T178 will work well in combination with rectangle R178.)

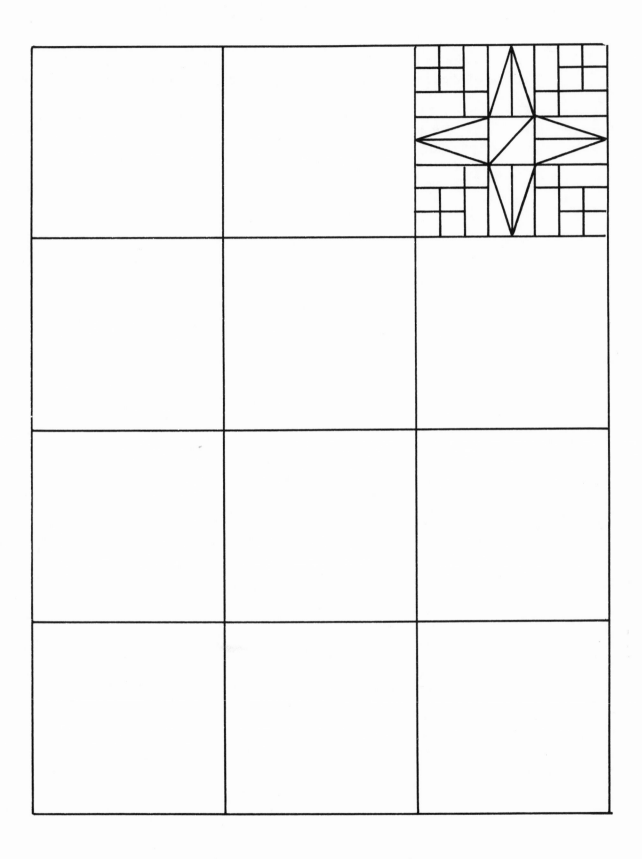

Determining the Number of Templates in the Quilt

Now you must count the number of times each template appears in each color in the quilt top. The worksheets provided will help you do this. Notice that if your quilt top design is based on the repetition of a single block design, you can determine the number of templates of each color in one block and multiply it by the number of blocks in the quilt top. On the other hand, if you are using an overall design, you must count each piece on the grid.

Once you have completed the worksheet, turn to the Yardage Charts Chapters and complete the yardage required by using the charts as explained there.

1	2	3	4	5		6	7	8
							Yardage required	
							36″	45″
Color	Template shape	Template Code	Number of this template in block	Number of blocks in quilt		Total number of this template		
1.				×	=			
				×	=			
				×	=			
				×	=			
2.				×	=			
				×	=			
				×	=			
				×	=			
3.				×	=			
				×	=			
				×	=			
				×	=			
4.				×	=			
				×	=			
				×	=			

Chapter 2

Making Templates

Of all the steps involved in making a quilt, making accurate template patterns is perhaps the most important in ensuring that the finished quilt will look like your original design. Because making a patchwork quilt means sewing many small pieces of fabric together to make a design, the template patterns which you use to trace and cut the fabric templates must be precisely made. Spending the time necessary to get the template measurements perfect will save you hours of frustration while you are piecing your quilt.

To make your template patterns, you will need the following supplies:

> 8 lines to the inch graph paper
> rubber cement
> 24-inch ruler
> razor blade knife (or single-edged razor blade)
> sharp pencil or marker
> stiff cardboard

To begin, write down the size of the templates you need to make your quilt.

You need one template pattern for each different size piece of fabric in your design. Because the template measurements are given for the size of the piece as it will be in the finished quilt, *you will have to add a seam allowance* to each side before using the pattern to trace and cut the pieces from the fabric. Using 8 lines to the inch graph paper makes this easy. Most graph paper is sold in $8\frac{1}{2}$ inch by 11 inch sheets, so if your template will be larger than this, tape several sheets together until you reach the required size. When you do this, be certain that you line up the graph paper perfectly so that the inch designations match.

Since each square equals $\frac{1}{8}$ inch, you can use the graph squares rather than the markings on the ruler as a guide.

The template measurements given in this book reflect only two sides of each template. The dotted lines on the illustrations below show you which measurements are given:

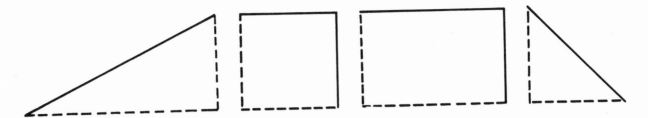

With your ruler, draw a line on the graph paper equal to one side of the template. After this line has been drawn, put your ruler perpendicular to the line at one end and draw the other measurement. To complete the first pattern, connect the lines you have just drawn to create the shape you need, whether a square, rectangle or triangle. This template should now match in width and length, the size of the piece *after* sewing.

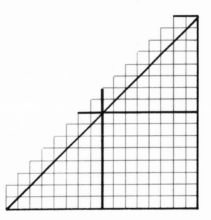

To add the ³/₈ inch seam allowance, simply count three squares outside the first two lines you drew and draw lines parallel to these lines. To complete the final template pattern, connect these new lines around the template. You should now have a template that measures ⁶/₈ inches more in width and length than the original measurements. For instance, if you began by drawing template code S5 (a square template measuring 3″ × 3″ when pieced), you should now have a template that measures 3⁶/₈″ × 3⁶/₈″.

Before we go to the next step, take your ruler and measure the template you've just drawn. If it is the precise shape you need, continue—if not, re-draw the template.

Since you will be tracing around the template several times, you will need to stiffen it so that it will retain its shape. One way to do this is to glue the graph paper to a sheet of stiff cardboard with rubber cement. Do this next, making sure that the graph paper is firmly affixed. Now, take your ruler and place it along the inside of the template pattern, almost touching the line on one side. Take your razor blade and cut this side of the template, using the ruler as a guide. Continue cutting along each side until your template pattern is complete.

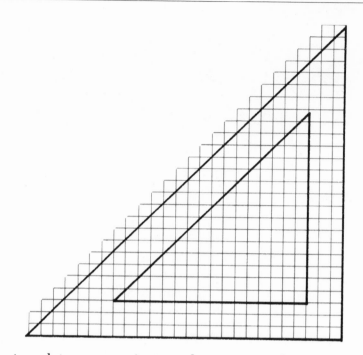

Measure the template once again to make sure it is the correct size.
The final test is to see if, by using the template, your fabric can be cut to the right size. So take a piece of the fabric and using the marker that you will use to trace all of the pieces, mark the fabric for cutting. Cut the fabric around the outline and measure the fabric piece. If it is correct—you've done it!

Chapter 3

Using The Yardage Charts

The yardage charts in this book are designed to eliminate fabric waste so that you will buy the exact amount of fabric you need of each color used in your quilt top.

There are four different chapters of charts—one each for square and rectangular templates and two for triangular templates (one for those triangles which are half of a square and one for triangles which are half of a rectangle).

Each chapter begins with a listing of the codes and measurements of the templates included in the charts. The measurements show the size of the template after it is sewn into the quilt top—therefore, the added seam allowance, while *included* in the yardage chart, is not shown in the listing. We have used a seam allowance of $3/8''$ in figuring out the charts.

If you need the yardage requirements for a template not listed in the book, simply use the chart for the template listed which is closest in size. For instance, if you have a square template which measures $5^1/4'' \times 5^1/4''$, use the yardage given for the $5^1/2'' \times 5^1/2''$ square.

Remember that the way in which you arrange the templates on the fabric will affect the number of pieces you can cut from the fabric. Here are some tips you can follow:

Wastage: We have allowed $1/4''$ between each template for wastage. We recommend that you cut each template separately so that the cut edge of one template does not become the cut edge of another template.

Triangular Templates: When using either kind of triangular templates, trace the templates with the first row right side up and the second row reversed, so that the templates in the two rows point toward each other. When you are using triangles which are based on one half of a rectangle, the template will have a right and wrong side, so be sure to keep the same surface of the template up when tracing the outline onto the fabric.

Template Placement: The number of rectangular or triangular templates (which are based on one half of a rectangle) that can be cut from a given amount of fabric will be effected by whether the short side or the long side of the template is placed parallel with the selvage. We have determined which placement is most efficient in each instance and have placed an asterick (*) next to the number when the templates should be placed with the long side along the selvage. The numbers without this sign indicate that the short side of the template should be placed along the selvage as illustrated below:

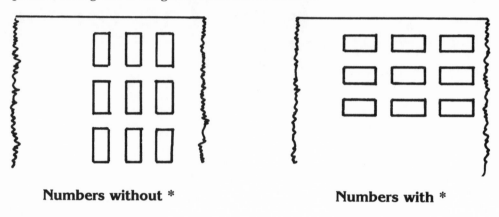

Numbers without *   **Numbers with ***

Using the Yardage Charts

To use the yardage charts in this book, simply look up the number of templates you will need for each color and template in your quilt and go to the left side of the chart where you will find the required yardage. Each chart gives the yardage for 36-inch and 45-inch wide fabric. It is a good idea to write down both yardage requirements before you go to the fabric store so that, regardless of the width, you will be able to economize on your fabric purchases.

For example, let's say we need 250 templates of template code R4. We would look at the charts until we found the one with template code R4 on the top. Then we would scan down the row until we came to the number 250. But there is no 250 on the chart. The nearest numbers are 240 and 270, so we would take the higher number and look to the left. We find that to make 250 templates of template code R4 we would need to buy 2.5 yards of 36″ wide fabric (and trace the template with the short side along the selvage) and 2 yards of 45″ wide fabric (and trace the template with the long side along the selvage).

36 " WIDE FABRIC

TEMPLATE CODES

YARDS	R1	R2	R3	R4	R5	R6	R7	R8
0.25	54*	36	28	24	20	18*	18*	12
0.50	108	81	63	54	45	36	36	27
0.75	162*	117	91	78	65	54*	54*	39
1.00	216	162	126	108	90	72	72	54
1.25	270*	198	162*	132	110	90*	90*	72*
1.50	324	243	189	162	135	108	108	90*
1.75	378*	279	217	186	162*	126*	126*	108*
2.00	432	324	252	216	180	162*	144	126*
2.25	486*	360	288*	240	200	180*	162*	144*
2.50	540	405	324*	270	225	198*	180	162*
2.75	594*	441	343	294	252*	216*	198*	162*
3.00	648	486	378	324	270	234*	216	180*
3.25	702*	522	414*	348	290	252*	234*	198*
3.50	756	567	450*	378	324*	270*	252	216*
3.75	810*	603	486*	402	342*	288*	270*	234*
4.00	864	648	504	432	360	324*	288	252*
4.25	918*	684	540*	456	380	342*	306*	270*
4.50	972	729	576*	486	414*	360*	324	288*
4.75	1026*	765	612*	510	432*	378*	342*	306*
5.00	1080	810	648*	540	450	396*	360	324*

45 " WIDE FABRIC

TEMPLATE CODES

YARDS	R1	R2	R3	R4	R5	R6	R7	R8
0.25	66*	44	36	28	24	22*	22*	16
0.50	135	99	81	66*	54	45	45	36
0.75	198*	143	117	91	78	66*	66*	52
1.00	270	198	162	132*	110*	90	90	72
1.25	330	242	198	154	132	110	110	88
1.50	405	297	243	198*	162	135	135	110*
1.75	465	341	279	220*	198*	155	155	132*
2.00	540	396	324	264*	220*	198*	180	154*
2.25	600	440	360	286*	242*	220*	200	176*
2.50	675	495	405	330*	270	242*	225	198*
2.75	735	539	441	352*	308*	264*	245	198*
3.00	810	594	486	396*	330*	286*	270	220*
3.25	870	638	522	418*	352*	308*	290	242*
3.50	945	693	567	462*	396*	330*	315	264*
3.75	1005	737	603	484*	418*	352*	335	286*
4.00	1080	792	648	528*	440*	396*	360	308*
4.25	1140	836	684	550*	462*	418*	380	330*
4.50	1215	891	729	594*	506*	440*	405	352*
4.75	1275	935	765	616*	528*	462*	425	374*
5.00	1350	990	810	660*	550*	484*	450	396*

Chapter 4

Yardage Charts: Square Templates

SQUARE TEMPLATE CODES AND MEASUREMENTS

TEMPLATE CODE	MEASUREMENT WITHOUT SEAM ALLOWANCE (IN INCHES)
S1	1 x 1
S2	1 1/2 x 1 1/2
S3	2 x 2
S4	2 1/2 x 2 1/2
S5	3 x 3
S6	3 1/2 x 3 1/2
S7	4 x 4
S8	4 1/2 x 4 1/2
S9	5 x 5
S10	5 1/2 x 5 1/2
S11	6 x 6
S12	6 1/2 x 6 1/2
S13	7 x 7
S14	7 1/2 x 7 1/2
S15	8 x 8
S16	8 1/2 x 8 1/2
S17	9 x 9
S18	9 1/2 x 9 1/2
S19	10 x 10
S20	10 1/2 x 10 1/2
S21	11 x 11
S22	11 1/2 x 11 1/2
S23	12 x 12
S24	12 1/2 X 12 1/2
S25	13 x 13
S26	13 1/2 x 13 1/2
S27	14 x 14
S28	14 1/2 x 14 1/2
S29	15 x 15
S30	15 1/2 x 15 1/2
S31	16 x 16
S32	16 1/2 x 16 1/2
S33	17 x 17
S34	17 1/2 x 17 1/2
S35	18 x 18
S36	18 1/2 x 18 1/2
S37	19 x 19
S38	19 1/2 x 19 1/2
S39	20 x 20
S40	20 1/2 x 20 1/2
S41	21 x 21

TEMPLATE CODE	MEASUREMENT WITHOUT SEAM ALLOWANCE (IN INCHES)
S42	21 1/2 × 21 1/2
S43	22 × 22
S44	22 1/2 × 22 1/2
S45	23 × 23
S46	23 1/2 × 23 1/2
S47	24 × 24
S48	24 1/2 × 24 1/2
S49	25 × 25

36 " WIDE FABRIC

TEMPLATE CODES

YARDS	S1	S2	S3	S4	S5	S6	S7	S8
0.25	72	42	36	20	18	16	7	6
0.50	162	98	72	50	36	32	21	18
0.75	234	140	108	70	54	48	35	24
1.00	324	196	144	100	81	64	49	36
1.25	396	252	180	120	99	80	63	48
1.50	486	294	216	150	117	96	70	54
1.75	558	350	252	180	135	112	84	66
2.00	648	392	288	200	162	128	98	78
2.25	720	448	324	230	180	144	112	84
2.50	810	504	360	250	198	160	126	96
2.75	882	546	396	280	216	176	133	108
3.00	972	602	432	300	243	192	147	114
3.25	1044	644	468	330	261	208	161	126
3.50	1134	700	504	360	279	224	175	132
3.75	1206	756	540	380	297	240	189	144
4.00	1296	798	576	410	324	256	196	156
4.25	1368	854	612	430	342	272	210	162
4.50	1458	896	648	460	360	288	224	174
4.75	1530	952	684	480	378	304	238	186
5.00	1620	1008	720	510	405	320	252	192

45 " WIDE FABRIC

TEMPLATE CODES

YARDS	S1	S2	S3	S4	S5	S6	S7	S8
0.25	88	54	45	24	22	20	9	8
0.50	198	126	90	60	44	40	27	24
0.75	286	180	135	84	66	60	45	32
1.00	396	252	180	120	99	80	63	48
1.25	484	324	225	144	121	100	81	64
1.50	594	378	270	180	143	120	90	72
1.75	682	450	315	216	165	140	108	88
2.00	792	504	360	240	198	160	126	104
2.25	880	576	405	276	220	180	144	112
2.50	990	648	450	300	242	200	162	128
2.75	1078	702	495	336	264	220	171	144
3.00	1188	774	540	360	297	240	189	152
3.25	1276	828	585	396	319	260	207	168
3.50	1386	900	630	432	341	280	225	176
3.75	1474	972	675	456	363	300	243	192
4.00	1584	1026	720	492	396	320	252	208
4.25	1672	1098	765	516	418	340	270	216
4.50	1782	1152	810	552	440	360	288	232
4.75	1870	1224	855	576	462	380	306	248
5.00	1980	1296	900	612	495	400	324	256

36 " WIDE FABRIC

TEMPLATE CODES

YARDS	S9	S10	S11	S12	S13	S14	S15	S16
0.25	6	5	5	4	4	4	4	0
0.50	18	10	10	8	8	8	8	3
0.75	24	20	15	12	12	12	12	6
1.00	36	25	25	16	16	16	16	9
1.25	42	30	30	24	20	20	20	12
1.50	54	40	35	28	24	24	24	15
1.75	60	45	45	32	28	28	28	18
2.00	72	55	50	36	36	32	32	21
2.25	78	60	55	40	40	36	36	24
2.50	90	65	60	48	44	40	40	27
2.75	96	75	70	52	48	44	44	30
3.00	108	80	75	56	52	48	48	33
3.25	114	90	80	60	56	52	52	36
3.50	126	95	90	64	60	56	56	39
3.75	132	100	95	72	64	60	60	42
4.00	144	110	100	76	72	64	64	45
4.25	150	115	105	80	76	72	68	48
4.50	162	120	115	84	80	76	72	51
4.75	168	130	120	88	84	80	76	54
5.00	180	135	125	96	88	84	80	54

45 " WIDE FABRIC

TEMPLATE CODES

YARDS	S9	S10	S11	S12	S13	S14	S15	S16
0.25	7	6	6	6	5	5	5	0
0.50	21	12	12	12	10	10	10	4
0.75	28	24	18	18	15	15	15	8
1.00	42	30	30	24	20	20	20	12
1.25	49	36	36	36	25	25	25	16
1.50	63	48	42	42	30	30	30	20
1.75	70	54	54	48	35	35	35	24
2.00	84	66	60	54	45	40	40	28
2.25	91	72	66	60	50	45	45	32
2.50	105	78	72	72	55	50	50	36
2.75	112	90	84	78	60	55	55	40
3.00	126	96	90	84	65	60	60	44
3.25	133	108	96	90	70	65	65	48
3.50	147	114	108	96	75	70	70	52
3.75	154	120	114	108	80	75	75	56
4.00	168	132	120	114	90	80	80	60
4.25	175	138	126	120	95	90	85	64
4.50	189	144	138	126	100	95	90	68
4.75	196	156	144	132	105	100	95	72
5.00	210	162	150	144	110	105	100	72

36 " WIDE FABRIC

TEMPLATE CODES

YARDS	S17	S18	S19	S20	S21	S22	S23	S24
0.25	0	0	0	0	0	0	0	0
0.50	3	3	3	3	3	2	2	2
0.75	6	6	6	6	6	4	4	4
1.00	9	9	9	9	9	4	4	4
1.25	12	12	12	9	9	6	6	6
1.50	15	15	12	12	12	8	8	8
1.75	18	18	15	15	15	10	8	8
2.00	21	18	18	18	18	10	10	10
2.25	24	21	21	21	18	12	12	12
2.50	27	24	24	21	21	14	12	12
2.75	27	27	27	24	24	14	14	14
3.00	30	30	27	27	27	16	16	16
3.25	33	33	30	30	27	18	18	16
3.50	36	36	33	30	30	20	18	18
3.75	39	36	36	33	33	20	20	20
4.00	42	39	39	36	36	22	22	20
4.25	45	42	39	39	36	24	22	22
4.50	48	45	42	42	39	24	24	24
4.75	51	48	45	42	42	26	26	24
5.00	54	51	48	45	45	28	26	26

45 " WIDE FABRIC

TEMPLATE CODES

YARDS	S17	S18	S19	S20	S21	S22	S23	S24
0.25	0	0	0	0	0	0	0	0
0.50	4	4	4	3	3	3	3	3
0.75	8	8	8	6	6	6	6	6
1.00	12	12	12	9	9	6	6	6
1.25	16	16	16	9	9	9	9	9
1.50	20	20	16	12	12	12	12	12
1.75	24	24	20	15	15	15	12	12
2.00	28	24	24	18	18	15	15	15
2.25	32	28	28	21	18	18	18	18
2.50	36	32	32	21	21	21	18	18
2.75	36	36	36	24	24	21	21	21
3.00	40	40	36	27	27	24	24	24
3.25	44	44	40	30	27	27	27	24
3.50	48	48	44	30	30	30	27	27
3.75	52	48	48	33	33	30	30	30
4.00	56	52	52	36	36	33	33	30
4.25	60	56	52	39	36	36	33	33
4.50	64	60	56	42	39	36	36	36
4.75	68	64	60	42	42	39	39	36
5.00	72	68	64	45	45	42	39	39

36 " WIDE FABRIC

TEMPLATE CODES

YARDS	S25	S26	S27	S28	S29	S30	S31	S32
0.25	0	0	0	0	0	0	0	0
0.50	2	2	2	2	2	2	2	2
0.75	2	2	2	2	2	2	2	2
1.00	4	4	4	4	4	4	4	4
1.25	6	6	6	4	4	4	4	4
1.50	6	6	6	6	6	6	6	6
1.75	8	8	8	8	6	6	6	6
2.00	10	8	8	8	8	8	8	8
2.25	10	10	10	10	10	8	8	8
2.50	12	12	12	10	10	10	10	10
2.75	14	12	12	12	12	12	10	10
3.00	14	14	14	12	12	12	12	12
3.25	16	16	14	14	14	14	12	12
3.50	18	16	16	16	14	14	14	14
3.75	18	18	18	16	16	16	14	14
4.00	20	18	18	18	18	16	16	16
4.25	20	20	20	18	18	18	18	16
4.50	22	22	20	20	20	18	18	18
4.75	24	22	22	22	20	20	20	18
5.00	24	24	24	22	22	20	20	20

45 " WIDE FABRIC

TEMPLATE CODES

YARDS	S25	S26	S27	S28	S29	S30	S31	S32
0.25	0	0	0	0	0	0	0	0
0.50	3	3	3	2	2	2	2	2
0.75	3	3	3	2	2	2	2	2
1.00	6	6	6	4	4	4	4	4
1.25	9	9	9	4	4	4	4	4
1.50	9	9	9	6	6	6	6	6
1.75	12	12	12	8	6	6	6	6
2.00	15	12	12	8	8	8	8	8
2.25	15	15	15	10	10	8	8	8
2.50	18	18	18	10	10	10	10	10
2.75	21	18	18	12	12	12	10	10
3.00	21	21	21	12	12	12	12	12
3.25	24	24	21	14	14	14	12	12
3.50	27	24	24	16	14	14	14	14
3.75	27	27	27	16	16	16	14	14
4.00	30	27	27	18	18	16	16	16
4.25	30	30	30	18	18	18	18	16
4.50	33	33	30	20	20	18	18	18
4.75	36	33	33	22	20	20	20	18
5.00	36	36	36	22	22	20	20	20

36 " WIDE FABRIC

TEMPLATE CODES

YARDS	S33	S34	S35	S36	S37	S38	S39	S40
0.25	0	0	0	0	0	0	0	0
0.50	2	0	0	0	0	0	0	0
0.75	2	1	1	1	1	1	1	1
1.00	4	1	1	1	1	1	1	1
1.25	4	2	2	2	2	2	2	2
1.50	6	2	2	2	2	2	2	2
1.75	6	3	3	3	3	3	3	2
2.00	8	3	3	3	3	3	3	3
2.25	8	4	4	4	4	3	3	3
2.50	10	4	4	4	4	4	4	4
2.75	10	5	5	5	4	4	4	4
3.00	12	5	5	5	5	5	5	5
3.25	12	6	6	6	5	5	5	5
3.50	14	6	6	6	6	6	6	5
3.75	14	7	7	6	6	6	6	6
4.00	16	7	7	7	7	7	6	6
4.25	16	8	8	7	7	7	7	7
4.50	18	8	8	8	8	7	7	7
4.75	18	9	9	8	8	8	8	7
5.00	20	9	9	9	9	8	8	8

45 " WIDE FABRIC

TEMPLATE CODES

YARDS	S33	S34	S35	S36	S37	S38	S39	S40
0.25	0	0	0	0	0	0	0	0
0.50	2	0	0	0	0	0	0	0
0.75	2	2	2	2	2	2	2	2
1.00	4	2	2	2	2	2	2	2
1.25	4	4	4	4	4	4	4	4
1.50	6	4	4	4	4	4	4	4
1.75	6	6	6	6	6	6	6	4
2.00	8	6	6	6	6	6	6	6
2.25	8	8	8	8	8	6	6	6
2.50	10	8	8	8	8	8	8	8
2.75	10	10	10	10	8	8	8	8
3.00	12	10	10	10	10	10	10	10
3.25	12	12	12	12	10	10	10	10
3.50	14	12	12	12	12	12	12	10
3.75	14	14	14	12	12	12	12	12
4.00	16	14	14	14	14	14	12	12
4.25	16	16	16	14	14	14	14	14
4.50	18	16	16	16	16	14	14	14
4.75	18	18	18	16	16	16	16	14
5.00	20	18	18	18	18	16	16	16

36 " WIDE FABRIC

TEMPLATE CODES

YARDS	S41	S42	S43	S44	S45	S46	S47	S48	S49
0.25	0	0	0	0	0	0	0	0	0
0.50	0	0	0	0	0	0	0	0	0
0.75	1	1	1	1	1	1	1	1	1
1.00	1	1	1	1	1	1	1	1	1
1.25	2	2	1	1	1	1	1	1	1
1.50	2	2	2	2	2	2	2	2	2
1.75	2	2	2	2	2	2	2	2	2
2.00	3	3	3	3	3	2	2	2	2
2.25	3	3	3	3	3	3	3	3	3
2.50	4	4	3	3	3	3	3	3	3
2.75	4	4	4	4	4	4	3	3	3
3.00	4	4	4	4	4	4	4	4	4
3.25	5	5	5	4	4	4	4	4	4
3.50	5	5	5	5	5	5	5	4	4
3.75	6	6	5	5	5	5	5	5	5
4.00	6	6	6	6	6	5	5	5	5
4.25	6	6	6	6	6	6	6	6	5
4.50	7	7	7	6	6	6	6	6	6
4.75	7	7	7	7	7	6	6	6	6
5.00	8	8	7	7	7	7	7	7	6

45 " WIDE FABRIC

TEMPLATE CODES

YARDS	S41	S42	S43	S44	S45	S46	S47	S48	S49
0.25	0	0	0	0	0	0	0	0	0
0.50	0	0	0	0	0	0	0	0	0
0.75	2	2	1	1	1	1	1	1	1
1.00	2	2	1	1	1	1	1	1	1
1.25	4	4	1	1	1	1	1	1	1
1.50	4	4	2	2	2	2	2	2	2
1.75	4	4	2	2	2	2	2	2	2
2.00	6	6	3	3	3	2	2	2	2
2.25	6	6	3	3	3	3	3	3	3
2.50	8	8	3	3	3	3	3	3	3
2.75	8	8	4	4	4	4	3	3	3
3.00	8	8	4	4	4	4	4	4	4
3.25	10	10	5	4	4	4	4	4	4
3.50	10	10	5	5	5	5	5	4	4
3.75	12	12	5	5	5	5	5	5	5
4.00	12	12	6	6	6	5	5	5	5
4.25	12	12	6	6	6	6	6	6	5
4.50	14	14	7	6	6	6	6	6	6
4.75	14	14	7	7	7	6	6	6	6
5.00	16	16	7	7	7	7	7	7	6

Chapter 5

Yardage Charts: Triangular Templates (Based on Squares)

TRIANGLE TEMPLATE CODES AND MEASUREMENTS
BASED ON SQUARES

TEMPLATE CODE	MEASUREMENT WITHOUT SEAM ALLOWANCE (IN INCHES)
TR1	1 x 1
TR2	1 1/2 x 1 1/2
TR3	2 x 2
TR4	2 1/2 x 2 1/2
TR5	3 x 3
TR6	3 1/2 x 3 1/2
TR7	4 x 4
TR8	4 1/2 x 4 1/2
TR9	5 x 5
TR10	5 1/2 x 5 1/2
TR11	6 x 6
TR12	6 1/2 x 6 1/2
TR13	7 x 7
TR14	7 1/2 x 7 1/2
TR15	8 x 8
TR16	8 1/2 x 8 1/2
TR17	9 x 9
TR18	9 1/2 x 9 1/2
TR19	10 x 10
TR20	10 1/2 x 10 1/2
TR21	11 x 11
TR22	11 1/2 x 11 1/2
TR23	12 x 12
TR24	12 1/2 X 12 1/2
TR25	13 x 13
TR26	13 1/2 x 13 1/2
TR27	14 x 14
TR28	14 1/2 x 14 1/2
TR29	15 x 15
TR30	15 1/2 x 15 1/2
TR31	16 x 16
TR32	16 1/2 x 16 1/2
TR33	17 x 17
TR34	17 1/2 x 17 1/2
TR35	18 x 18
TR36	18 1/2 x 18 1/2
TR37	19 x 19
TR38	19 1/2 x 19 1/2
TR39	20 x 20
TR40	20 1/2 x 20 1/2
TR41	21 x 21

TEMPLATE CODE	MEASUREMENT WITHOUT SEAM ALLOWANCE (IN INCHES)
TR42	21 1/2 × 21 1/2
TR43	22 × 22
TR44	22 1/2 × 22 1/2
TR45	23 × 23
TR46	23 1/2 × 23 1/2
TR47	24 × 24
TR48	24 1/2 × 24 1/2
TR49	25 × 25

36 " WIDE FABRIC

TEMPLATE CODES

YARDS	TR1	TR2	TR3	TR4	TR5	TR6	TR7	TR8
0.25	78	44	36	32	14	12	12	10
0.50	156	110	72	64	42	36	36	20
0.75	234	176	126	96	70	60	48	40
1.00	338	242	162	128	98	72	72	50
1.25	416	308	216	160	126	96	84	70
1.50	494	352	252	192	154	120	108	80
1.75	598	418	288	224	182	144	132	100
2.00	676	484	342	272	210	156	144	110
2.25	754	550	378	304	238	180	168	130
2.50	858	616	432	336	266	204	180	140
2.75	936	660	468	368	294	228	204	150
3.00	1014	726	522	400	308	240	216	170
3.25	1118	792	558	432	336	264	240	180
3.50	1196	858	594	464	364	288	264	200
3.75	1274	924	648	512	392	300	276	210
4.00	1378	968	684	544	420	324	300	230
4.25	1456	1034	738	576	448	348	312	240
4.50	1534	1100	774	608	476	372	336	260
4.75	1638	1166	828	640	504	384	348	270
5.00	1716	1232	864	672	532	408	372	280

45 " WIDE FABRIC

TEMPLATE CODES

YARDS	TR1	TR2	TR3	TR4	TR5	TR6	TR7	TR8
0.25	96	56	48	40	18	16	14	14
0.50	192	140	96	80	54	48	42	28
0.75	288	224	168	120	90	80	56	56
1.00	416	308	216	160	126	96	84	70
1.25	512	392	288	200	162	128	98	98
1.50	608	448	336	240	198	160	126	112
1.75	736	532	384	280	234	192	154	140
2.00	832	616	456	340	270	208	168	154
2.25	928	700	504	380	306	240	196	182
2.50	1056	784	576	420	342	272	210	196
2.75	1152	840	624	460	378	304	238	210
3.00	1248	924	696	500	396	320	252	238
3.25	1376	1008	744	540	432	352	280	252
3.50	1472	1092	792	580	468	384	308	280
3.75	1568	1176	864	640	504	400	322	294
4.00	1696	1232	912	680	540	432	350	322
4.25	1792	1316	984	720	576	464	364	336
4.50	1888	1400	1032	760	612	496	392	364
4.75	2016	1484	1104	800	648	512	406	378
5.00	2112	1568	1152	840	684	544	434	392

36 " WIDE FABRIC

TEMPLATE CODES

YARDS	TR9	TR10	TR11	TR12	TR13	TR14	TR15	TR16
0.25	10	8	8	8	8	0	0	0
0.50	20	16	16	16	16	6	6	6
0.75	40	24	24	24	24	12	12	12
1.00	50	32	32	32	32	18	18	18
1.25	60	48	40	40	40	24	24	24
1.50	80	56	56	48	48	30	30	30
1.75	90	64	64	56	56	36	36	36
2.00	100	72	72	64	64	42	42	42
2.25	120	88	80	72	72	48	48	42
2.50	130	96	88	80	80	54	54	48
2.75	140	104	96	96	88	60	60	54
3.00	160	112	112	104	96	66	66	60
3.25	170	128	120	112	104	72	72	66
3.50	180	136	128	120	112	78	72	72
3.75	200	144	136	128	120	84	78	78
4.00	210	152	144	136	128	90	84	84
4.25	220	168	152	144	136	96	90	84
4.50	240	176	168	152	144	102	96	90
4.75	250	184	176	160	152	108	102	96
5.00	260	192	184	168	160	114	108	102

45 " WIDE FABRIC

TEMPLATE CODES

YARDS	TR9	TR10	TR11	TR12	TR13	TR14	TR15	TR16
0.25	12	12	10	10	10	0	0	0
0.50	24	24	20	20	20	8	8	8
0.75	48	36	30	30	30	16	16	16
1.00	60	48	40	40	40	24	24	24
1.25	72	72	50	50	50	32	32	32
1.50	96	84	70	60	60	40	40	40
1.75	108	96	80	70	70	48	48	48
2.00	120	108	90	80	80	56	56	56
2.25	144	132	100	90	90	64	64	56
2.50	156	144	110	100	100	72	72	64
2.75	168	156	120	120	110	80	80	72
3.00	192	168	140	130	120	88	88	80
3.25	204	192	150	140	130	96	96	88
3.50	216	204	160	150	140	104	96	96
3.75	240	216	170	160	150	112	104	104
4.00	252	228	180	170	160	120	112	112
4.25	264	252	190	180	170	128	120	112
4.50	288	264	210	190	180	136	128	120
4.75	300	276	220	200	190	144	136	128
5.00	312	288	230	210	200	152	144	136

36 " WIDE FABRIC

TEMPLATE CODES

YARDS	TR17	TR18	TR19	TR20	TR21	TR22	TR23	TR24
0.25	0	0	0	0	0	0	0	0
0.50	6	6	6	4	4	4	4	4
0.75	12	12	12	8	8	8	4	4
1.00	18	18	18	8	8	8	8	8
1.25	24	24	18	12	12	12	12	12
1.50	30	24	24	16	16	16	12	12
1.75	30	30	30	20	16	16	16	16
2.00	36	36	36	20	20	20	20	20
2.25	42	42	36	24	24	24	20	20
2.50	48	48	42	28	28	24	24	24
2.75	54	48	48	32	28	28	28	24
3.00	60	54	54	32	32	32	28	28
3.25	60	60	54	36	36	32	32	32
3.50	66	66	60	40	36	36	36	32
3.75	72	72	66	44	40	40	36	36
4.00	78	72	72	44	44	40	40	40
4.25	84	78	78	48	48	44	44	40
4.50	90	84	78	52	48	48	44	44
4.75	90	90	84	56	52	48	48	48
5.00	96	96	90	56	56	52	52	48

45 " WIDE FABRIC

TEMPLATE CODES

YARDS	TR17	TR18	TR19	TR20	TR21	TR22	TR23	TR24
0.25	0	0	0	0	0	0	0	0
0.50	8	8	6	6	6	6	6	6
0.75	16	16	12	12	12	12	6	6
1.00	24	24	18	12	12	12	12	12
1.25	32	32	18	18	18	18	18	18
1.50	40	32	24	24	24	24	18	18
1.75	40	40	30	30	24	24	24	24
2.00	48	48	36	30	30	30	30	30
2.25	56	56	36	36	36	36	30	30
2.50	64	64	42	42	42	36	36	36
2.75	72	64	48	48	42	42	42	36
3.00	80	72	54	48	48	48	42	42
3.25	80	80	54	54	54	48	48	48
3.50	88	88	60	60	54	54	54	48
3.75	96	96	66	66	60	60	54	54
4.00	104	96	72	66	66	60	60	60
4.25	112	104	78	72	72	66	66	60
4.50	120	112	78	78	72	72	66	66
4.75	120	120	84	84	78	72	72	72
5.00	128	128	90	84	84	78	78	72

36 " WIDE FABRIC

TEMPLATE CODES

YARDS	TR25	TR26	TR27	TR28	TR29	TR30	TR31	TR32
0.25	0	0	0	0	0	0	0	0
0.50	4	4	4	4	4	4	4	0
0.75	4	4	4	4	4	4	4	2
1.00	8	8	8	8	8	8	8	2
1.25	12	8	8	8	8	8	8	4
1.50	12	12	12	12	12	12	12	4
1.75	16	16	16	12	12	12	12	6
2.00	16	16	16	16	16	16	16	6
2.25	20	20	20	16	16	16	16	8
2.50	24	20	20	20	20	20	20	8
2.75	24	24	24	24	20	20	20	10
3.00	28	28	24	24	24	24	24	10
3.25	28	28	28	28	28	24	24	12
3.50	32	32	32	28	28	28	28	12
3.75	36	32	32	32	32	28	28	14
4.00	36	36	36	32	32	32	32	14
4.25	40	40	36	36	36	32	32	16
4.50	44	40	40	36	36	36	36	16
4.75	44	44	40	40	40	36	36	18
5.00	48	44	44	44	40	40	40	18

45 " WIDE FABRIC

TEMPLATE CODES

YARDS	TR25	TR26	TR27	TR28	TR29	TR30	TR31	TR32
0.25	0	0	0	0	0	0	0	0
0.50	6	4	4	4	4	4	4	0
0.75	6	4	4	4	4	4	4	4
1.00	12	8	8	8	8	8	8	4
1.25	18	8	8	8	8	8	8	8
1.50	18	12	12	12	12	12	12	8
1.75	24	16	16	12	12	12	12	12
2.00	24	16	16	16	16	16	16	12
2.25	30	20	20	16	16	16	16	16
2.50	36	20	20	20	20	20	20	16
2.75	36	24	24	24	20	20	20	20
3.00	42	28	24	24	24	24	24	20
3.25	42	28	28	28	28	24	24	24
3.50	48	32	32	28	28	28	28	24
3.75	54	32	32	32	32	28	28	28
4.00	54	36	36	32	32	32	32	28
4.25	60	40	36	36	36	32	32	32
4.50	66	40	40	36	36	36	36	32
4.75	66	44	40	40	40	36	36	36
5.00	72	44	44	44	40	40	40	36

36 " WIDE FABRIC

TEMPLATE CODES

YARDS	TR33	TR34	TR35	TR36	T37	TR38	TR39	TR40
0.25	0	0	0	0	0	0	0	0
0.50	0	0	0	0	0	0	0	0
0.75	2	2	2	2	2	2	2	2
1.00	2	2	2	2	2	2	2	2
1.25	4	4	4	4	4	4	4	4
1.50	4	4	4	4	4	4	4	4
1.75	6	6	6	6	6	4	4	4
2.00	6	6	6	6	6	6	6	6
2.25	8	8	8	8	6	6	6	6
2.50	8	8	8	8	8	8	8	8
2.75	10	10	10	8	8	8	8	8
3.00	10	10	10	10	10	10	8	8
3.25	12	12	10	10	10	10	10	10
3.50	12	12	12	12	12	10	10	10
3.75	14	14	12	12	12	12	12	12
4.00	14	14	14	14	12	12	12	12
4.25	16	14	14	14	14	14	14	12
4.50	16	16	16	16	14	14	14	14
4.75	18	16	16	16	16	16	14	14
5.00	18	18	18	16	16	16	16	16

45 " WIDE FABRIC

TEMPLATE CODES

YARDS	TR33	TR34	TR35	TR36	T37	TR38	TR39	TR40
0.25	0	0	0	0	0	0	0	0
0.50	0	0	0	0	0	0	0	0
0.75	4	4	4	4	4	4	4	4
1.00	4	4	4	4	4	4	4	4
1.25	8	8	8	8	8	8	8	8
1.50	8	8	8	8	8	8	8	8
1.75	12	12	12	12	12	8	8	8
2.00	12	12	12	12	12	12	12	12
2.25	16	16	16	16	12	12	12	12
2.50	16	16	16	16	16	16	16	16
2.75	20	20	20	16	16	16	16	16
3.00	20	20	20	20	20	20	16	16
3.25	24	24	20	20	20	20	20	20
3.50	24	24	24	24	24	20	20	20
3.75	28	28	24	24	24	24	24	24
4.00	28	28	28	28	24	24	24	24
4.25	32	28	28	28	28	28	28	24
4.50	32	32	32	32	28	28	28	28
4.75	36	32	32	32	32	32	28	28
5.00	36	36	36	32	32	32	32	32

36 " WIDE FABRIC

TEMPLATE CODES

YARDS	TR41	TR42	TR43	TR44	TR45	TR46	TR47	TR48	TR49
0.25	0	0	0	0	0	0	0	0	0
0.50	0	0	0	0	0	0	0	0	0
0.75	2	2	2	2	2	2	2	2	2
1.00	2	2	2	2	2	2	2	2	2
1.25	2	2	2	2	2	2	2	2	2
1.50	4	4	4	4	4	4	4	4	4
1.75	4	4	4	4	4	4	4	4	4
2.00	6	6	6	4	4	4	4	4	4
2.25	6	6	6	6	6	6	6	6	6
2.50	6	6	6	6	6	6	6	6	6
2.75	8	8	8	8	8	6	6	6	6
3.00	8	8	8	8	8	8	8	8	8
3.25	10	10	8	8	8	8	8	8	8
3.50	10	10	10	10	10	8	8	8	8
3.75	10	10	10	10	10	10	10	10	10
4.00	12	12	12	10	10	10	10	10	10
4.25	12	12	12	12	12	12	10	10	10
4.50	14	12	12	12	12	12	12	12	12
4.75	14	14	14	14	12	12	12	12	12
5.00	14	14	14	14	14	14	14	12	12

45 " WIDE FABRIC

TEMPLATE CODES

YARDS	TR41	TR42	TR43	TR44	TR45	TR46	TR47	TR48	TR49
0.25	0	0	0	0	0	0	0	0	0
0.50	0	0	0	0	0	0	0	0	0
0.75	2	2	2	2	2	2	2	2	2
1.00	2	2	2	2	2	2	2	2	2
1.25	2	2	2	2	2	2	2	2	2
1.50	4	4	4	4	4	4	4	4	4
1.75	4	4	4	4	4	4	4	4	4
2.00	6	6	6	4	4	4	4	4	4
2.25	6	6	6	6	6	6	6	6	6
2.50	6	6	6	6	6	6	6	6	6
2.75	8	8	8	8	8	6	6	6	6
3.00	8	8	8	8	8	8	8	8	8
3.25	10	10	8	8	8	8	8	8	8
3.50	10	10	10	10	10	8	8	8	8
3.75	10	10	10	10	10	10	10	10	10
4.00	12	12	12	10	10	10	10	10	10
4.25	12	12	12	12	12	12	10	10	10
4.50	14	12	12	12	12	12	12	12	12
4.75	14	14	14	14	12	12	12	12	12
5.00	14	14	14	14	14	14	14	12	12

Chapter 6

Yardage Charts: Rectangular Templates

RECTANGLE TEMPLATE CODES AND MEASUREMENTS

TEMPLATE CODE	MEASUREMENT WITHOUT SEAM ALLOWANCE (IN INCHES)
R1	1 × 2
R2	1 × 3
R3	1 × 4
R4	1 × 5
R5	1 × 6
R6	1 × 7
R7	1 × 8
R8	1 × 9
R9	1 × 10
R10	1 × 11
R11	1 × 12
R12	1 × 13
R13	1 × 14
R14	1 × 15
R15	1 × 16
R16	1 × 17
R17	1 × 18
R18	1 × 19
R19	1 × 20
R20	1 × 21
R21	1 × 22
R22	1 × 23
R23	1 × 24
R24	1 × 25
R25	1 1/2 × 2 1/2
R26	1 1/2 × 3 1/2
R27	1 1/2 × 4 1/2
R28	1 1/2 × 5 1/2
R29	1 1/2 × 6 1/2
R30	1 1/2 × 7 1/2
R31	1 1/2 × 8 1/2
R32	1 1/2 × 9 1/2
R33	1 1/2 × 10 1/2
R34	1 1/2 × 11 1/2
R35	1 1/2 × 12 1/2
R36	1 1/2 × 13 1/2
R37	1 1/2 × 14 1/2
R38	1 1/2 × 15 1/2
R39	1 1/2 × 16 1/2
R40	1 1/2 × 17 1/2
R41	1 1/2 × 18 1/2

TEMPLATE CODE	MEASUREMENT WITHOUT SEAM ALLOWANCE (IN INCHES)
R42	1 1/2 × 19 1/2
R43	1 1/2 × 20 1/2
R44	1 1/2 × 21 1/2
R45	1 1/2 × 22 1/2
R46	1 1/2 × 23 1/2
R47	1 1/2 × 24 1/2
R48	2 × 4
R49	2 × 5
R50	2 × 6
R51	2 × 7
R52	2 × 8
R53	2 × 9
R54	2 × 10
R55	2 × 11
R56	2 × 12
R57	2 × 13
R58	2 × 14
R59	2 × 15
R60	2 × 16
R61	2 × 17
R62	2 × 18
R63	2 × 19
R64	2 × 20
R65	2 × 21
R66	2 × 22
R67	2 × 23
R68	2 × 24
R69	2 × 25
R70	2 1/2 × 4 1/2
R71	2 1/2 × 5 1/2
R72	2 1/2 × 6 1/2
R73	2 1/2 × 7 1/2
R74	2 1/2 × 8 1/2
R75	2 1/2 × 9 1/2
R76	2 1/2 × 10 1/2
R77	2 1/2 × 11 1/2
R78	2 1/2 × 12 1/2
R79	2 1/2 × 13 1/2
R80	2 1/2 × 14 1/2
R81	2 1/2 × 15 1/2
R82	2 1/2 × 16 1/2

TEMPLATE CODE	MEASUREMENT WITHOUT SEAM ALLOWANCE (IN INCHES)
R83	2 1/2 × 17 1/2
R84	2 1/2 × 18 1/2
R85	2 1/2 × 19 1/2
R86	2 1/2 × 20 1/2
R87	2 1/2 × 21 1/2
R88	2 1/2 × 22 1/2
R89	2 1/2 × 23 1/2
R90	2 1/2 × 24 1/2
R91	3 × 5
R92	3 × 6
R93	3 × 7
R94	3 × 8
R95	3 × 9
R96	3 × 10
R97	3 × 11
R98	3 × 12
R99	3 × 13
R100	3 × 14
R101	3 × 15
R102	3 × 16
R103	3 × 17
R104	3 × 18
R105	3 × 19
R106	3 × 20
R107	3 × 21
R108	3 × 22
R109	3 × 23
R110	3 × 24
R111	3 × 25
R112	3 1/2 × 5 1/2
R113	3 1/2 × 6 1/2
R114	3 1/2 × 7 1/2
R115	3 1/2 × 8 1/2
R116	3 1/2 × 9 1/2
R117	3 1/2 × 10 1/2
R118	3 1/2 × 11 1/2
R119	3 1/2 × 12 1/2
R120	3 1/2 × 13 1/2
R121	3 1/2 × 14 1/2
R122	3 1/2 × 15 1/2
R123	3 1/2 × 16 1/2

TEMPLATE CODE	MEASUREMENT WITHOUT SEAM ALLOWANCE (IN INCHES)
R124	3 1/2 × 17 1/2
R125	3 1/2 × 18 1/2
R126	3 1/2 × 19 1/2
R127	3 1/2 × 20 1/2
R128	3 1/2 × 21 1/2
R129	3 1/2 × 22 1/2
R130	3 1/2 × 23 1/2
R131	3 1/2 × 24 1/2
R132	4 × 6
R133	4 × 7
R134	4 × 8
R135	4 × 9
R136	4 × 10
R137	4 × 11
R138	4 × 12
R139	4 × 13
R140	4 × 14
R141	4 × 15
R142	4 × 16
R143	4 × 17
R144	4 × 18
R145	4 × 19
R146	4 × 20
R147	4 × 21
R148	4 × 22
R149	4 × 23
R150	4 × 24
R151	4 × 25
R152	4 1/2 × 6 1/2
R153	4 1/2 × 7 1/2
R154	4 1/2 × 8 1/2
R155	4 1/2 × 9 1/2
R156	4 1/2 × 10 1/2
R157	4 1/2 × 11 1/2
R158	4 1/2 × 12 1/2
R159	4 1/2 × 13 1/2
R160	4 1/2 × 14 1/2
R161	4 1/2 × 15 1/2
R162	4 1/2 × 16 1/2
R163	4 1/2 × 17 1/2
R164	4 1/2 × 18 1/2

TEMPLATE CODE	MEASUREMENT WITHOUT SEAM ALLOWANCE (IN INCHES)
R165	4 1/2 × 19 1/2
R166	4 1/2 × 20 1/2
R167	4 1/2 × 21 1/2
R168	4 1/2 × 22 1/2
R169	4 1/2 × 23 1/2
R170	4 1/2 × 24 1/2
R171	5 × 7
R172	5 × 8
R173	5 × 9
R174	5 × 10
R175	5 × 11
R176	5 × 12
R177	5 × 13
R178	5 × 14
R179	5 × 15
R180	5 × 16
R181	5 × 17
R182	5 × 18
R183	5 × 19
R184	5 × 20
R185	5 × 21
R186	5 × 22
R187	5 × 23
R188	5 × 24
R189	5 × 25
R190	5 1/2 × 7 1/2
R191	5 1/2 × 8 1/2
R192	5 1/2 × 9 1/2
R193	5 1/2 × 10 1/2
R194	5 1/2 × 11 1/2
R195	5 1/2 × 12 1/2
R196	5 1/2 × 13 1/2
R197	5 1/2 × 14 1/2
R198	5 1/2 × 15 1/2
R199	5 1/2 × 16 1/2
R200	5 1/2 × 17 1/2
R201	5 1/2 × 18 1/2
R202	5 1/2 × 19 1/2
R203	5 1/2 × 20 1/2
R204	5 1/2 × 21 1/2
R205	5 1/2 × 22 1/2

TEMPLATE CODE	MEASUREMENT WITHOUT SEAM ALLOWANCE (IN INCHES)
R206	5 1/2 x 23 1/2
R207	5 1/2 x 24 1/2
R208	6 x 8
R209	6 x 9
R210	6 x 10
R211	6 x 11
R212	6 x 12
R213	6 x 13
R214	6 x 14
R215	6 x 15
R216	6 x 16
R217	6 x 17
R218	6 x 18
R219	6 x 19
R220	6 x 20
R221	6 x 21
R222	6 x 22
R223	6 x 23
R224	6 x 24
R225	6 x 25
R226	6 1/2 x 8 1/2
R227	6 1/2 x 9 1/2
R228	6 1/2 x 10 1/2
R229	6 1/2 x 11 1/2
R230	6 1/2 x 12 1/2
R231	6 1/2 x 13 1/2
R232	6 1/2 x 14 1/2
R233	6 1/2 x 15 1/2
R234	6 1/2 x 16 1/2
R235	6 1/2 x 17 1/2
R236	6 1/2 x 18 1/2
R237	6 1/2 x 19 1/2
R238	6 1/2 x 20 1/2
R239	6 1/2 x 21 1/2
R240	6 1/2 x 22 1/2
R241	6 1/2 x 23 1/2
R242	6 1/2 x 24 1/2
R243	7 x 9
R244	7 x 10
R245	7 x 11
R246	7 x 12

TEMPLATE CODE	MEASUREMENT WITHOUT SEAM ALLOWANCE (IN INCHES)
R247	7 × 13
R248	7 × 14
R249	7 × 15
R250	7 × 16
R251	7 × 17
R252	7 × 18
R253	7 × 19
R254	7 × 20
R255	7 × 21
R256	7 × 22
R257	7 × 23
R258	7 × 24
R259	7 × 25
R260	7 1/2 × 9 1/2
R261	7 1/2 × 10 1/2
R262	7 1/2 × 11 1/2
R263	7 1/2 × 12 1/2
R264	7 1/2 × 13 1/2
R265	7 1/2 × 14 1/2
R266	7 1/2 × 15 1/2
R267	7 1/2 × 16 1/2
R268	7 1/2 × 17 1/2
R269	7 1/2 × 18 1/2
R270	7 1/2 × 19 1/2
R271	7 1/2 × 20 1/2
R272	7 1/2 × 21 1/2
R273	7 1/2 × 22 1/2
R274	7 1/2 × 23 1/2
R275	7 1/2 × 24 1/2
R276	8 × 10
R277	8 × 11
R278	8 × 12
R279	8 × 13
R280	8 × 14
R281	8 × 15
R282	8 × 16
R283	8 × 17
R284	8 × 18
R285	8 × 19
R286	8 × 20
R287	8 × 21

TEMPLATE CODE	MEASUREMENT WITHOUT SEAM ALLOWANCE (IN INCHES)
R288	8 × 22
R289	8 × 23
R290	8 × 24
R291	8 × 25
R292	8 1/2 × 10 1/2
R293	8 1/2 × 11 1/2
R294	8 1/2 × 12 1/2
R295	8 1/2 × 13 1/2
R296	8 1/2 × 14 1/2
R297	8 1/2 × 15 1/2
R298	8 1/2 × 16 1/2
R299	8 1/2 × 17 1/2
R300	8 1/2 × 18 1/2
R301	8 1/2 × 19 1/2
R302	8 1/2 × 20 1/2
R303	8 1/2 × 21 1/2
R304	8 1/2 × 22 1/2
R305	8 1/2 × 23 1/2
R306	8 1/2 × 24 1/2
R307	9 × 12
R308	9 × 13
R309	9 × 14
R310	9 × 15
R311	9 × 16
R312	9 × 17
R313	9 × 18
R314	9 × 19
R315	9 × 20
R316	9 × 21
R317	9 × 22
R318	9 × 23
R319	9 × 24
R320	9 × 25
R321	9 1/2 × 12 1/2
R322	9 1/2 × 13 1/2
R323	9 1/2 × 14 1/2
R324	9 1/2 × 15 1/2
R325	9 1/2 × 16 1/2
R326	9 1/2 × 17 1/2
R327	9 1/2 × 18 1/2
R328	9 1/2 × 19 1/2

TEMPLATE CODE	MEASUREMENT WITHOUT SEAM ALLOWANCE (IN INCHES)
R329	9 1/2 × 20 1/2
R330	9 1/2 × 21 1/2
R331	9 1/2 × 22 1/2
R332	9 1/2 × 23 1/2
R333	9 1/2 × 24 1/2
R334	10 × 12
R335	10 × 13
R336	10 × 14
R337	10 × 15
R338	10 × 16
R339	10 × 17
R340	10 × 18
R341	10 × 19
R342	10 × 20
R343	10 × 21
R344	10 × 22
R345	10 × 23
R346	10 × 24
R347	10 × 25

36 " WIDE FABRIC

TEMPLATE CODES

YARDS	R1	R2	R3	R4	R5	R6	R7	R8
0.25	54*	36	28	24	20	18*	18*	12
0.50	108	81	63	54	45	36	36	27
0.75	162*	117	91	78	65	54*	54*	39
1.00	216	162	126	108	90	72	72	54
1.25	270*	198	162*	132	110	90*	90*	72*
1.50	324	243	189	162	135	108	108	90*
1.75	378*	279	217	186	162*	126*	126*	108*
2.00	432	324	252	216	180	162*	144	126*
2.25	486*	360	288*	240	200	180*	162*	144*
2.50	540	405	324*	270	225	198*	180	162*
2.75	594*	441	343	294	252*	216*	198*	162*
3.00	648	486	378	324	270	234*	216	180*
3.25	702*	522	414*	348	290	252*	234*	198*
3.50	756	567	450*	378	324*	270*	234*	198*
3.75	810*	603	486*	402	342*	288*	270*	234*
4.00	864	648	504	432	360	324*	288	252*
4.25	918*	684	540*	456	380	342*	306*	270*
4.50	972	729	576*	486	414*	360*	324	288*
4.75	1026*	765	612*	510	432*	378*	342*	306*
5.00	1080	810	648*	540	450	396*	360	324*

45 " WIDE FABRIC

TEMPLATE CODES

YARDS	R1	R2	R3	R4	R5	R6	R7	R8
0.25	66*	44	36	28	24	22*	22*	16
0.50	135	99	81	66*	54	45	45	36
0.75	198*	143	117	91	78	66*	66*	52
1.00	270	198	162	132*	110*	90	90	72
1.25	330	242	198	154	132	110	110	88
1.50	405	297	243	198*	162	135	135	88
1.75	465	341	279	220*	198*	155	155	110*
2.00	540	396	324	264*	220*	198*	180	154*
2.25	600	440	360	286*	242*	220*	200	176*
2.50	675	495	405	330*	270	242*	225	198*
2.75	735	539	441	352*	308*	264*	245	198*
3.00	810	594	486	396*	330*	286*	270	220*
3.25	870	638	522	418*	352*	286*	270	220*
3.50	945	693	567	462*	396*	330*	315	242*
3.75	1005	737	603	484*	418*	352*	335	286*
4.00	1080	792	648	528*	440*	396*	360	308*
4.25	1140	836	684	550*	462*	418*	380	330*
4.50	1215	891	729	594*	506*	440*	405	352*
4.75	1275	935	765	616*	528*	462*	425	352*
5.00	1350	990	810	660*	550*	484*	450	396*

36 " WIDE FABRIC

TEMPLATE CODES

YARDS	R9	R10	R11	R12	R13	R14	R15	R16
0.25	12	12	8	8	8	8	8	8
0.50	27	27	18	18	18	18	18	18
0.75	39	39	36*	26	26	26	26	26
1.00	54	54	36	36	36	36	36	36
1.25	72*	66	54*	54*	54*	44	44	44
1.50	81	81	72*	54	54	54	54	54
1.75	93	93	72*	72*	72*	62	62	62
2.00	108	108	90*	90*	72	72	72	72
2.25	126*	120	108*	90*	90*	90*	80	80
2.50	144*	135	108*	108*	108*	90	90	90
2.75	162*	147	126*	126*	108*	108*	98	98
3.00	162	162	144*	126*	126*	108	108	108
3.25	180*	174	162*	144*	126*	126*	116	116
3.50	198*	189	162*	162*	144*	126	126	126
3.75	216*	201	180*	162*	162*	144*	134	134
4.00	234*	216	198*	180*	162*	162*	144	144
4.25	234*	228	198*	180*	180*	162*	162*	152
4.50	252*	243	216*	198*	180*	180*	162	162
4.75	270*	255	234*	216*	198*	180*	180*	170
5.00	288*	270	234*	216*	216*	198*	180	180

45 " WIDE FABRIC

TEMPLATE CODES

YARDS	R9	R10	R11	R12	R13	R14	R15	R16
0.25	16	12	12	12	12	8	8	8
0.50	36	27	27	27	27	22*	22*	22*
0.75	52	44*	44*	39	39	26	26	26
1.00	72	66*	54	54	54	44*	44*	44*
1.25	88	66	66	66	66	44	44	44
1.50	108	88*	88*	81	81	66*	66*	66*
1.75	124	110*	93	93	93	66*	66*	66*
2.00	144	132*	110*	110*	108	88*	88*	88*
2.25	160	132*	132*	120	120	110*	88*	88*
2.50	180	154*	135	135	135	110*	110*	110*
2.75	198*	176*	154*	154*	147	132*	110*	110*
3.00	216	198*	176*	162	162	132*	132*	132*
3.25	232	198*	198*	176*	174	154*	132*	132*
3.50	252	220*	198*	198*	189	154*	154*	154*
3.75	268	242*	220*	201	201	176*	154*	154*
4.00	288	264*	242*	220*	216	198*	176*	176*
4.25	304	264*	242*	228	228	198*	198*	176*
4.50	324	286*	264*	243	243	220*	198*	198*
4.75	340	308*	286*	264*	255	220*	220*	198*
5.00	360	330*	286*	270	270	242*	220*	220*

36 " WIDE FABRIC

TEMPLATE CODES

YARDS	R17	R18	R19	R20	R21	R22	R23	R24
0.25	4	4	4	4	4	4	4	4
0.50	9	9	9	9	9	9	9	9
0.75	18*	18*	18*	18*	18*	18*	18*	18*
1.00	18	18	18	18	18	18	18	18
1.25	36*	36*	36*	36*	22	22	22	22
1.50	36*	36*	36*	36*	36*	36*	36*	36*
1.75	54*	54*	54*	36*	36*	36*	36*	36*
2.00	54*	54*	54*	54*	54*	54*	36	36
2.25	72*	72*	54*	54*	54*	54*	54*	54*
2.50	72*	72*	72*	72*	54*	54*	54*	54*
2.75	90*	72*	72*	72*	72*	72*	54*	54*
3.00	90*	90*	90*	72*	72*	72*	72*	72*
3.25	108*	90*	90*	90*	90*	72*	72*	72*
3.50	108*	108*	108*	90*	90*	90*	90*	72*
3.75	126*	108*	108*	108*	90*	90*	90*	90*
4.00	126*	126*	108*	108*	108*	108*	90*	90*
4.25	144*	126*	126*	108*	108*	108*	108*	90*
4.50	144*	144*	126*	126*	126*	108*	108*	108*
4.75	162*	144*	144*	126*	126*	126*	108*	108*
5.00	162*	162*	144*	144*	126*	126*	126*	108*

45 " WIDE FABRIC

TEMPLATE CODES

YARDS	R17	R18	R19	R20	R21	R22	R23	R24
0.25	8	8	8	8	4	4	4	4
0.50	18	18	18	18	9	9	9	9
0.75	26	26	26	26	22*	22*	22*	22*
1.00	36	36	36	36	22*	22*	22*	22*
1.25	44	44	44	44	22	22	22	22
1.50	54	54	54	54	44*	44*	44*	44*
1.75	66*	66*	66*	62	44*	44*	44*	44*
2.00	72	72	72	72	66*	66*	44*	44*
2.25	88*	88*	80	80	66*	66*	66*	66*
2.50	90	90	90	90	66*	66*	66*	66*
2.75	110*	98	98	98	88*	88*	66*	66*
3.00	110*	110*	110*	108	88*	88*	88*	88*
3.25	132*	116	116	116	110*	88*	88*	88*
3.50	132*	132*	132*	126	110*	110*	110*	88*
3.75	154*	134	134	134	110*	110*	110*	110*
4.00	154*	154*	144	144	132*	132*	110*	110*
4.25	176*	154*	154*	152	132*	132*	132*	110*
4.50	176*	176*	162	162	154*	132*	132*	132*
4.75	198*	176*	176*	170	154*	154*	132*	132*
5.00	198*	198*	180	180	154*	154*	154*	132*

36 " WIDE FABRIC

TEMPLATE CODES

YARDS	R25	R26	R27	R28	R29	R30	R31	R32
0.25	30	28*	18	15	14*	14*	9	9
0.50	70	56	42	35	28	28	21	21
0.75	100	84*	60	56*	42*	42*	30	30
1.00	140	112	84	70	56	56	42	42
1.25	180	144	112*	90	84*	72	56*	56*
1.50	210	168	126	112*	98*	84	70*	70*
1.75	252*	200	154*	126*	112*	100	84*	84*
2.00	280	224	182*	154*	126*	112	98*	84
2.25	322*	256	196*	168*	140*	128	112*	98*
2.50	360	288	224*	182*	168*	144	126*	112*
2.75	392*	312	252*	210*	182*	156	140*	126*
3.00	430	344	266*	224*	196*	172	154*	140*
3.25	462*	368	294*	252*	210*	184	168*	154*
3.50	504*	400	308*	266*	224*	200	182*	168*
3.75	540	432	336*	280*	252*	216	196*	168*
4.00	574*	456	364*	308*	266*	228	210*	182*
4.25	610	488	378*	322*	280*	252*	224*	196*
4.50	644*	512	406*	336*	294*	266*	238*	210*
4.75	680	544	434*	364*	308*	280*	252*	224*
5.00	720	576	448*	378*	336*	294*	252*	238*

45 " WIDE FABRIC

TEMPLATE CODES

YARDS	R25	R26	R27	R28	R29	R30	R31	R32
0.25	36	36*	24	18	18	18*	12	12
0.50	90*	72*	56	42	42	36*	28	28
0.75	126*	108*	80	72*	60	54*	40	40
1.00	180*	144*	112	90*	84	72*	56	56
1.25	216	180	144	108	108	90	72	72
1.50	270*	216*	168	144*	126	108*	90*	90*
1.75	324*	252*	200	162*	150	126*	108*	108*
2.00	360*	288*	234*	198*	168	144*	126*	112
2.25	414*	324*	256	216*	192	162*	144*	128
2.50	450*	360	288	234*	216	180	162*	144
2.75	504*	396*	324*	270*	234	198*	180*	162*
3.00	540*	432*	344	288*	258	216*	198*	180*
3.25	594*	468*	378*	324*	276	234*	216*	198*
3.50	648*	504*	400	342*	300	252*	234*	216*
3.75	684*	540	432	360*	324	270	252*	216
4.00	738*	576*	468*	396*	342	288*	270*	234*
4.25	774*	612*	488	414*	366	324*	288*	252*
4.50	828*	648*	522*	432*	384	342*	306*	270*
4.75	864*	684*	558*	468*	408	360*	324*	288*
5.00	918*	720	576	486*	432	378*	324*	306*

36 " WIDE FABRIC

TEMPLATE CODES

YARDS	R33	R34	R35	R36	R37	R38	R39	R40
0.25	9	6	6	6	6	6	6	3
0.50	21	14	14	14	14	14	14	7
0.75	30	28*	28*	20	20	20	20	14*
1.00	42	28	28	28	28	28	28	14
1.25	54	42*	42*	42*	36	36	36	28*
1.50	63	56*	56*	42	42	42	42	28*
1.75	75	70*	56*	56*	56*	50	50	42*
2.00	84	70*	70*	56	56	56	56	42*
2.25	98*	84*	84*	70*	70*	64	64	56*
2.50	108	98*	84*	84*	72	72	72	56*
2.75	117	98*	98*	84*	84*	84*	78	70*
3.00	129	112*	112*	98*	86	86	86	70*
3.25	140*	126*	112*	112*	98*	98*	92	84*
3.50	150	140*	126*	112*	112*	100	100	84*
3.75	162	140*	140*	126*	112*	112*	108	98*
4.00	171	154*	140*	126*	126*	114	114	98*
4.25	183	168*	154*	140*	126*	126*	122	112*
4.50	196*	168*	168*	154*	140*	128	128	112*
4.75	204	182*	168*	154*	154*	140*	136	126*
5.00	216	196*	182*	168*	154*	144	144	126*

45 " WIDE FABRIC

TEMPLATE CODES

YARDS	R33	R34	R35	R36	R37	R38	R39	R40
0.25	9	9	9	9	6	6	6	6
0.50	21	21	21	21	18*	18*	18*	14
0.75	36*	36*	36*	30	20	20	20	20
1.00	54*	42	42	42	36*	36*	36*	28
1.25	54	54	54	54	36	36	36	36
1.50	72*	72*	72*	63	54*	54*	54*	42
1.75	90*	90*	75	75	72	54*	54*	54*
2.00	108*	90*	90*	84	72	72*	72*	56
2.25	126*	108*	108*	96	90*	72*	72*	72*
2.50	126*	126*	108	108	90*	90*	90*	72
2.75	144*	126*	126*	117	108*	108*	90*	90*
3.00	162*	144*	144*	129	108*	108*	108*	90*
3.25	180*	162*	144*	144*	126*	126*	108*	108*
3.50	180*	180*	162*	150	144*	126*	126*	108*
3.75	198*	180*	180*	162	144*	144*	126*	126*
4.00	216*	198*	180*	171	162*	144*	144*	126*
4.25	234*	216*	198*	183	162*	162*	144*	144*
4.50	252*	216*	216*	198*	180*	162*	162*	144*
4.75	252*	234*	216*	204	198*	180*	162*	162*
5.00	270*	252*	234*	216	198*	180*	180*	162*

36 " WIDE FABRIC

TEMPLATE CODES

YARDS	R41	R42	R43	R44	R45	R46	R47	R48
0.25	3	3	3	3	3	3	3	21
0.50	7	7	7	7	7	7	7	42
0.75	14*	14*	14*	14*	14*	14*	14*	63
1.00	14	14	14	14	14	14	14	84
1.25	28*	28*	28*	28*	18	18	18	108*
1.50	28*	28*	28*	28*	28*	28*	28*	126
1.75	42*	42*	28*	28*	28*	28*	28*	147
2.00	42*	42*	42*	42*	42*	28	28	168
2.25	56*	42*	42*	42*	42*	42*	42*	192*
2.50	56*	56*	56*	56*	42*	42*	42*	216*
2.75	70*	56*	56*	56*	56*	56*	42*	231
3.00	70*	70*	70*	56*	56*	56*	56*	252
3.25	84*	70*	70*	70*	56*	56*	56*	276*
3.50	84*	84*	70*	70*	70*	70*	56*	300*
3.75	84*	84*	84*	84*	70*	70*	70*	324*
4.00	98*	98*	84*	84*	84*	70*	70*	336
4.25	98*	98*	98*	84*	84*	84*	84*	360*
4.50	112*	98*	98*	98*	84*	84*	84*	384*
4.75	112*	112*	98*	98*	98*	84*	84*	408*
5.00	126*	112*	112*	112*	98*	98*	98*	432*

45 " WIDE FABRIC

TEMPLATE CODES

YARDS	R41	R42	R43	R44	R45	R46	R47	R48
0.25	6	6	6	6	3	3	3	27
0.50	14	14	14	14	7	7	7	54
0.75	20	20	20	20	18*	18*	18*	81
1.00	28	28	28	28	18*	18*	18*	108
1.25	36	36	36	36	18	18	18	135
1.50	42	42	42	42	36*	36*	36*	162
1.75	54*	54*	50	50	36*	36*	36*	189
2.00	56	56	56	56	54*	36*	36*	216
2.25	72*	64	64	64	54*	54*	54*	243
2.50	72	72	72	72	54*	54*	54*	270
2.75	90*	78	78	78	72*	72*	54*	297
3.00	90*	90*	90*	86	72*	72*	72*	324
3.25	108*	92	92	92	72*	72*	72*	351
3.50	108*	108*	100	100	90*	90*	72*	378
3.75	108	108	108	108	90*	90*	90*	405
4.00	126*	126*	114	114	108*	90*	90*	432
4.25	126*	126*	126*	122	108*	108*	108*	459
4.50	144*	128	128	128	108*	108*	108*	486
4.75	144*	144*	136	136	126*	108*	108*	513
5.00	162*	144	144	144	126*	126*	126*	540

36 " WIDE FABRIC

TEMPLATE CODES

YARDS	R49	R50	R51	R52	R53	R54	R55	R56
0.25	18	15	12	12	9	9	9	6
0.50	36	30	24	24	18	18	18	12
0.75	54	45	36	36	27	27	27	24*
1.00	72	60	48	48	36	36	36	24
1.25	90	75	60	60	48*	48*	45	36*
1.50	108	90	72	72	60*	54	54	48*
1.75	126	108*	84	84	72*	63	63	48*
2.00	144	120	108*	96	84*	72	72	60*
2.25	162	135	120*	108	96*	84*	81	72*
2.50	180	150	132*	120	108*	96*	90	72*
2.75	198	168*	144*	132	108*	108*	99	84*
3.00	216	180	156*	144	120*	108	108	96*
3.25	234	195	168*	156	132*	120*	117	108*
3.50	252	216*	180*	168	144*	132*	126	108*
3.75	270	228*	192*	180	156*	144*	135	120*
4.00	288	240	216*	192	168*	156*	144	132*
4.25	306	255	228*	204	180*	156*	153	132*
4.50	324	276*	240*	216	192*	168*	162	144*
4.75	342	288*	252*	228	204*	180*	171	156*
5.00	360	300	264*	240	216*	192*	180	156*

45 " WIDE FABRIC

TEMPLATE CODES

YARDS	R49	R50	R51	R52	R53	R54	R55	R56
0.25	21	18	15	15	12	12	9	9
0.50	45*	36	30	30	24	24	18	18
0.75	63	54	45	45	36	36	30*	30*
1.00	90*	75*	60	60	48	48	45*	36
1.25	105	90	75	75	60	60	45	45
1.50	135*	108	90	90	75*	72	60*	60*
1.75	150*	135*	105	105	90*	84	75*	63
2.00	180*	150*	135*	120	105*	96	90*	75*
2.25	195*	165*	150*	135	120*	108	90*	90*
2.50	225*	180	165*	150	135*	120	105*	90
2.75	240*	210*	180*	165	135*	135*	120*	105*
3.00	270*	225*	195*	180	150*	144	135*	120*
3.25	285*	240*	210*	195	165*	156	135*	135*
3.50	315*	270*	225*	210	180*	168	150*	135*
3.75	330*	285*	240*	225	195*	180	165*	150*
4.00	360*	300*	270*	240	210*	195*	180*	165*
4.25	375*	315*	285*	255	225*	204	180*	165*
4.50	405*	345*	300*	270	240*	216	195*	180*
4.75	420*	360*	315*	285	255*	228	210*	195*
5.00	450*	375*	330*	300	270*	240	225*	195*

36 " WIDE FABRIC

TEMPLATE CODES

YARDS	R57	R58	R59	R60	R61	R62	R63	R64
0.25	6	6	6	6	6	3	3	3
0.50	12	12	12	12	12	6	6	6
0.75	18	18	18	18	18	12*	12*	12*
1.00	24	24	24	24	24	12	12	12
1.25	36*	36*	30	30	30	24*	24*	24*
1.50	36	36	36	36	36	24*	24*	24*
1.75	48*	48*	42	42	42	36*	36*	36*
2.00	60*	48	48	48	48	36*	36*	36*
2.25	60*	60*	60*	54	54	48*	48*	36*
2.50	72*	72*	60	60	60	48*	48*	48*
2.75	84*	72*	72*	66	66	60*	48*	48*
3.00	84*	84*	72	72	72	60*	60*	60*
3.25	96*	84*	84*	78	78	72*	60*	60*
3.50	108*	96*	84	84	84	72*	72*	72*
3.75	108*	108*	96*	90	90	84*	72*	72*
4.00	120*	108*	108*	96	96	84*	84*	72*
4.25	120*	120*	108*	108*	102	96*	84*	84*
4.50	132*	120*	120*	108	108	96*	96*	84*
4.75	144*	132*	120*	120*	114	108*	96*	96*
5.00	144*	144*	132*	120	120	108*	108*	96*

45 " WIDE FABRIC

TEMPLATE CODES

YARDS	R57	R58	R59	R60	R61	R62	R63	R64
0.25	9	9	6	6	6	6	6	6
0.50	18	18	15*	15*	15*	12	12	12
0.75	27	27	18	18	18	18	18	18
1.00	36	36	30*	30*	30*	24	24	24
1.25	45	45	30	30	30	30	30	30
1.50	54	54	45*	45*	45*	36	36	36
1.75	63	63	45*	45*	45*	45*	45*	45*
2.00	75*	72	60*	60*	60*	48	48	48
2.25	81	81	75*	60*	60*	60*	60*	54
2.50	90	90	75*	75*	75*	60	60	60
2.75	105*	99	90*	75*	75*	75*	66	66
3.00	108	108	90*	90*	90*	75*	75*	75*
3.25	120*	117	105*	90*	90*	90*	78	78
3.50	135*	126	105*	105*	105*	90*	90*	90*
3.75	135	135	120*	105*	105*	105*	90	90
4.00	150*	144	135*	120*	120*	105*	105*	96
4.25	153	153	135*	135*	120*	120*	105*	105*
4.50	165*	162	150*	135*	135*	120*	120*	108
4.75	180*	171	150*	150*	135*	135*	120*	120*
5.00	180	180	165*	150*	150*	135*	135*	120

36 " WIDE FABRIC

TEMPLATE CODES

YARDS	R65	R66	R67	R68	R69	R70	R71	R72
0.25	3	3	3	3	3	12	10	10✳
0.50	6	6	6	6	6	30	25	20
0.75	12✳	12✳	12✳	12✳	12✳	42	40✳	30✳
1.00	12	12	12	12	12	60	50	40
1.25	24✳	15	15	15	15	80✳	60	60✳
1.50	24✳	24✳	24✳	24✳	24✳	90	80✳	70✳
1.75	24✳	24✳	24✳	24✳	24✳	110✳	90	80✳
2.00	36✳	36✳	36✳	24	24	130✳	110✳	90✳
2.25	36✳	36✳	36✳	36✳	36✳	140✳	120✳	100✳
2.50	48✳	36✳	36✳	36✳	36✳	160✳	130✳	120✳
2.75	48✳	48✳	48✳	36✳	36✳	180✳	150✳	130✳
3.00	48✳	48✳	48✳	48✳	48✳	190✳	160✳	140✳
3.25	60✳	60✳	48✳	48✳	48✳	210✳	180✳	150✳
3.50	60✳	60✳	60✳	60✳	48✳	220✳	190✳	160✳
3.75	72✳	60✳	60✳	60✳	60✳	240✳	200✳	180✳
4.00	72✳	72✳	72✳	60✳	60✳	260✳	220✳	190✳
4.25	72✳	72✳	72✳	72✳	60✳	270✳	230✳	200✳
4.50	84✳	84✳	72✳	72✳	72✳	290✳	240✳	210✳
4.75	84✳	84✳	84✳	72✳	72✳	310✳	260✳	220✳
5.00	96✳	84✳	84✳	84✳	72✳	320✳	270✳	240✳

45 " WIDE FABRIC

TEMPLATE CODES

YARDS	R65	R66	R67	R68	R69	R70	R71	R72
0.25	6	3	3	3	3	16	12	12
0.50	12	6	6	6	6	40	30	30
0.75	18	15✳	15✳	15✳	15✳	56	48✳	42
1.00	24	15✳	15✳	15✳	15✳	80	60	60
1.25	30	15	15	15	15	96	72	72
1.50	36	30✳	30✳	30✳	30✳	120	96✳	90
1.75	42	30✳	30✳	30✳	30✳	144	108	108
2.00	48	45✳	45✳	30✳	30✳	160	132✳	120
2.25	54	45✳	45✳	45✳	45✳	184	144✳	138
2.50	60	45✳	45✳	45✳	45✳	200	156✳	150
2.75	66	60✳	60✳	45✳	45✳	224	180✳	168
3.00	72	60✳	60✳	60✳	60✳	240	192✳	180
3.25	78	75✳	60✳	60✳	60✳	264	216✳	198
3.50	84	75✳	75✳	75✳	60✳	288	228✳	216
3.75	90	75✳	75✳	75✳	75✳	304	240✳	228
4.00	96	90✳	90✳	75✳	75✳	328	264✳	246
4.25	102	90✳	90✳	90✳	75✳	344	276✳	258
4.50	108	105✳	90✳	90✳	90✳	368	288✳	276
4.75	114	105✳	105✳	90✳	90✳	384	312✳	288
5.00	120	105✳	105✳	105✳	90✳	408	324✳	306

36 " WIDE FABRIC

TEMPLATE CODES

YARDS	R73	R74	R75	R76	R77	R78	R79	R80
0.25	10*	6	6	6	4	4	4	4
0.50	20	15	15	15	10	10	10	10
0.75	30*	21	21	21	20*	20*	14	14
1.00	40	30	30	30	20	20	20	20
1.25	50*	40*	40*	36	30*	30*	30*	24
1.50	60	50*	50*	45	40*	40*	30	30
1.75	72	60*	60*	54	50*	40*	40*	40*
2.00	80	70*	60	60	50*	50*	40	40
2.25	92	80*	70*	70*	60*	60*	50*	50*
2.50	100	90*	80*	75	70*	60*	60*	50
2.75	112	100*	90*	84	70*	70*	60*	60*
3.00	120	110*	100*	90	80*	80*	70*	60
3.25	132	120*	110*	100*	90*	80*	80*	70*
3.50	144	130*	120*	108	100*	90*	80*	80*
3.75	152	140*	120*	114	100*	100*	90*	80*
4.00	164	150*	130*	123	110*	100*	90*	90*
4.25	180*	160*	140*	130*	120*	110*	100*	90*
4.50	190*	170*	150*	140*	120*	120*	110*	100*
4.75	200*	180*	160*	144	130*	120*	110*	110*
5.00	210*	180*	170*	153	140*	130*	120*	110*

45 " WIDE FABRIC

TEMPLATE CODES

YARDS	R73	R74	R75	R76	R77	R78	R79	R80
0.25	12*	8	8	6	6	6	6	4
0.50	25	20	20	15	15	15	15	12*
0.75	36*	28	28	24*	24*	24*	21	14
1.00	50	40	40	36*	30	30	30	24*
1.25	60	48	48	36	36	36	36	24
1.50	75	60	60	48*	48*	48*	45	36*
1.75	90	72	72	60*	60*	54	54	48*
2.00	100	84*	80	72*	60	60	60	48*
2.25	115	96*	92	84*	72*	72*	69	60*
2.50	125	108*	100	84*	84*	75	75	60*
2.75	140	120*	112	96*	84	84	84	72*
3.00	150	132*	120	108*	96*	96*	90	72*
3.25	165	144*	132	120*	108*	99	99	84*
3.50	180	156*	144	120*	120*	108	108	96*
3.75	190	168*	152	132*	120*	120*	114	96*
4.00	205	180*	164	144*	132*	123	123	108*
4.25	216*	192*	172	156*	144*	132*	129	108*
4.50	230	204*	184	168*	144*	144*	138	120*
4.75	240	216*	192	168*	156*	144	144	132*
5.00	255	216*	204	180*	168*	156*	153	132*

36 " WIDE FABRIC

TEMPLATE CODES

YARDS	R81	R82	R83	R84	R85	R86	R87	R88
0.25	4	4	2	2	2	2	2	2
0.50	10	10	5	5	5	5	5	5
0.75	14	14	10*	10*	10*	10*	10*	10*
1.00	20	20	10	10	10	10	10	10
1.25	24	24	20*	20*	20*	20*	20*	12
1.50	30	30	20*	20*	20*	20*	20*	20*
1.75	36	36	30*	30*	30*	20*	20*	20*
2.00	40	40	30*	30*	30*	30*	30*	30*
2.25	46	46	40*	40*	30*	30*	30*	30*
2.50	50	50	40*	40*	40*	40*	40*	30*
2.75	60*	56	50*	50*	40*	40*	40*	40*
3.00	60	60	50*	50*	50*	50*	40*	40*
3.25	70*	66	60*	60*	50*	50*	50*	40*
3.50	72	72	60*	60*	60*	50*	50*	50*
3.75	80*	76	70*	60*	60*	60*	60*	50*
4.00	82	82	70*	70*	70*	60*	60*	60*
4.25	90*	86	80*	70*	70*	70*	60*	60*
4.50	92	92	80*	80*	70*	70*	70*	60*
4.75	100*	96	90*	80*	80*	70*	70*	70*
5.00	102	102	90*	90*	80*	80*	80*	70*

45 " WIDE FABRIC

TEMPLATE CODES

YARDS	R81	R82	R83	R84	R85	R86	R87	R88
0.25	4	4	4	4	4	4	4	2
0.50	12*	12*	10	10	10	10	10	5
0.75	14	14	14	14	14	14	14	12*
1.00	24*	24*	20	20	20	20	20	12*
1.25	24	24	24	24	24	24	24	12
1.50	36*	36*	30	30	30	30	30	24*
1.75	36	36	36	36	36	36	36	24*
2.00	48*	48*	40	40	40	40	40	36*
2.25	48*	48*	48*	48*	46	46	46	36*
2.50	60*	60*	50	50	50	50	50	36*
2.75	72*	60*	60*	60*	56	56	56	48*
3.00	72*	72*	60	60	60	60	60	48*
3.25	84*	72*	72*	72*	66	66	66	48*
3.50	84*	84*	72	72	72	72	72	60*
3.75	96*	84*	84*	76	76	76	76	60*
4.00	96*	96*	84*	84*	84*	82	82	72*
4.25	108*	96*	96*	86	86	86	86	72*
4.50	108*	108*	96*	96*	92	92	92	72*
4.75	120*	108*	108*	96	96	96	96	84*
5.00	120*	120*	108*	108*	102	102	102	84*

36 " WIDE FABRIC

TEMPLATE CODES

YARDS	R89	R90	R91	R92	R93	R94	R95	R96
0.25	2	2	12	10	9*	9*	6	6
0.50	5	5	27*	20	18*	18*	12	12
0.75	10*	10*	36	30	27*	27*	18	18
1.00	10	10	54	45	36	36	27	27
1.25	12	12	66	55	45*	45*	36*	36*
1.50	20*	20*	81*	65	54*	54*	45*	39
1.75	20*	20*	90	81*	63*	63*	54*	45
2.00	20	20	108	90	81*	72	63*	54
2.25	30*	30*	120	100	90*	81*	72*	63*
2.50	30*	30*	135*	110	99*	90*	81*	72*
2.75	40*	30*	144	126*	108*	99*	81*	81*
3.00	40*	40*	162	135	117*	108	90*	81
3.25	40*	40*	174	145	126*	117*	99*	90*
3.50	50*	40*	189*	162*	135*	126*	108*	99*
3.75	50*	50*	198	171*	144*	135*	117*	108*
4.00	50*	50*	216	180	162*	144	126*	117*
4.25	60*	60*	228	190	171*	153*	135*	117*
4.50	60*	60*	243*	207*	180*	162*	144*	126*
4.75	60*	60*	252	216*	189*	171*	153*	135*
5.00	70*	70*	270	225	198*	180	162*	144*

45 " WIDE FABRIC

TEMPLATE CODES

YARDS	R89	R90	R91	R92	R93	R94	R95	R96
0.25	2	2	14	12	11*	11*	8	8
0.50	5	5	33*	24	22*	22*	16	16
0.75	12*	12*	44*	36	33*	33*	24	24
1.00	12*	12*	66*	55*	45	45	36	36
1.25	12	12	77	66	55	55	44	44
1.50	24*	24*	99*	78	66*	66*	55*	52
1.75	24*	24*	110*	99*	77*	77*	66*	60
2.00	24*	24*	132*	110*	99*	90	77*	72
2.25	36*	36*	143*	121*	110*	100	88*	80
2.50	36*	36*	165*	132	121*	110	99*	88
2.75	48*	36*	176*	154*	132*	121*	99*	99*
3.00	48*	48*	198*	165*	143*	135	110*	108
3.25	48*	48*	209*	176*	154*	145	121*	116
3.50	60*	48*	231*	198*	165*	155	132*	124
3.75	60*	60*	242*	209*	176*	165	143*	132
4.00	60*	60*	264*	220*	198*	180	154*	144
4.25	72*	72*	275*	231*	209*	190	165*	152
4.50	72*	72*	297*	253*	220*	200	176*	160
4.75	72*	72*	308*	264*	231*	210	187*	168
5.00	84*	84*	330*	275*	242*	225	198*	180

36 " WIDE FABRIC

TEMPLATE CODES

YARDS	R97	R98	R99	R100	R101	R102	R103	R104
0.25	6	4	4	4	4	4	4	2
0.50	12	9※	9※	9※	9※	9※	9※	4
0.75	18	18※	12	12	12	12	12	9※
1.00	27	18	18	18	18	18	18	9
1.25	33	27※	27※	27※	22	22	22	18※
1.50	39	36※	27※	27※	27※	27※	27※	18※
1.75	45	36※	36※	36※	30	30	30	27※
2.00	54	45※	45※	36	36	36	36	27※
2.25	60	54※	45※	45※	45※	40	40	36※
2.50	66	54※	54※	54※	45※	45※	45※	36※
2.75	72	63※	63※	54※	54※	48	48	45※
3.00	81	72※	63※	63※	54	54	54	45※
3.25	87	81※	72※	63※	63※	58	58	54※
3.50	93	81※	81※	72※	63※	63※	63※	54※
3.75	99	90※	81※	81※	72※	66	66	63※
4.00	108	99※	90※	81※	81※	72	72	63※
4.25	114	99※	90※	90※	81※	81※	76	72※
4.50	120	108※	99※	90※	90※	81※	81※	72※
4.75	126	117※	108※	99※	90※	90※	84	81※
5.00	135	117※	108※	108※	99※	90	90	81※

45 " WIDE FABRIC

TEMPLATE CODES

YARDS	R97	R98	R99	R100	R101	R102	R103	R104
0.25	6	6	6	6	4	4	4	4
0.50	12	12	12	12	11※	11※	11※	8
0.75	22※	22※	18	18	12	12	12	12
1.00	33※	27	27	27	22※	22※	22※	18
1.25	33	33	33	33	22	22	22	22
1.50	44※	44※	39	39	33※	33※	33※	26
1.75	55※	45	45	45	33※	33※	33※	33※
2.00	66※	55※	55※	54	44※	44※	44※	36
2.25	66※	66※	60	60	55※	44※	44※	44※
2.50	77※	66	66	66	55※	55※	55※	44
2.75	88※	77※	77※	72	66※	55※	55※	55※
3.00	99※	88※	81	81	66※	66※	66※	55※
3.25	99※	99※	88※	87	77※	66※	66※	66※
3.50	110※	99※	99※	93	77※	77※	77※	66※
3.75	121※	110※	99	99	88※	77※	77※	77※
4.00	132※	121※	110※	108	99※	88※	88※	77※
4.25	132※	121※	114	114	99※	99※	88※	88※
4.50	143※	132※	121※	120	110※	99※	99※	88※
4.75	154※	143※	132※	126	110※	110※	99※	99※
5.00	165※	143※	135	135	121※	110※	110※	99※

36 " WIDE FABRIC

TEMPLATE CODES

YARDS	R105	R106	R107	R108	R109	R110	R111	R112
0.25	2	2	2	2	2	2	2	10
0.50	4	4	4	4	4	4	4	20
0.75	9*	9*	9*	9*	9*	9*	9*	32*
1.00	9	9	9	9	9	9	9	40
1.25	18*	18*	18*	11	11	11	11	50
1.50	18*	18*	18*	18*	18*	18*	18*	64*
1.75	27*	27*	18*	18*	18*	18*	18*	72*
2.00	27*	27*	27*	27*	27*	18	18	88*
2.25	36*	27*	27*	27*	27*	27*	27*	96*
2.50	36*	36*	36*	27*	27*	27*	27*	104*
2.75	36*	36*	36*	36*	36*	27*	27*	120*
3.00	45*	45*	36*	36*	36*	36*	36*	128*
3.25	45*	45*	45*	45*	36*	36*	36*	144*
3.50	54*	54*	45*	45*	45*	45*	36*	152*
3.75	54*	54*	54*	45*	45*	45*	45*	160*
4.00	63*	54*	54*	54*	54*	45*	45*	176*
4.25	63*	63*	54*	54*	54*	54*	45*	184*
4.50	72*	63*	63*	63*	54*	54*	54*	192*
4.75	72*	72*	63*	63*	63*	54*	54*	208*
5.00	81*	72*	72*	63*	63*	63*	54*	216*

45 " WIDE FABRIC

TEMPLATE CODES

YARDS	R105	R106	R107	R108	R109	R110	R111	R112
0.25	4	4	4	2	2	2	2	12
0.50	8	8	8	4	4	4	4	24
0.75	12	12	12	11*	11*	11*	11*	40*
1.00	18	18	18	11*	11*	11*	11*	50*
1.25	22	22	22	11	11	11	11	60
1.50	26	26	26	22*	22*	22*	22*	80*
1.75	33*	33*	30	22*	22*	22*	22*	90*
2.00	36	36	36	33*	33*	22*	22*	110*
2.25	44*	40	40	33*	33*	33*	33*	120*
2.50	44	44	44	33*	33*	33*	33*	130*
2.75	48	48	48	44*	44*	33*	33*	150*
3.00	55*	55*	54	44*	44*	44*	44*	160*
3.25	58	58	58	55*	44*	44*	44*	180*
3.50	66*	66*	62	55*	55*	55*	44*	190*
3.75	66	66	66	55*	55*	55*	55*	200*
4.00	77*	72	72	66*	66*	55*	55*	220*
4.25	77*	77*	76	66*	66*	66*	55*	230*
4.50	88*	80	80	77*	66*	66*	66*	240*
4.75	88*	88*	84	77*	77*	66*	66*	260*
5.00	99*	90	90	77*	77*	77*	66*	270*

36 " WIDE FABRIC

TEMPLATE CODES

YARDS	R113	R114	R115	R116	R117	R118	R119	R120
0.25	8	8	6	6	6	4	4	4
0.50	16	16	12	12	12	8	8	8
0.75	24	24	18	18	18	16*	16*	12
1.00	32	32	24	24	24	16	16	16
1.25	48*	40	32*	32*	30	24*	24*	24*
1.50	56*	48	40*	40*	36	32*	32*	24
1.75	64*	56	48*	48*	42	40*	32*	32*
2.00	72*	64	56*	48	48	40*	40*	32
2.25	80*	72	64*	56*	56*	48*	48*	40*
2.50	96*	80	72*	64*	60	56*	48*	48*
2.75	104*	88	80*	72*	66	56*	56*	48*
3.00	112*	96	88*	80*	72	64*	64*	56*
3.25	120*	104	96*	88*	80*	72*	64*	64*
3.50	128*	112	104*	96*	84	80*	72*	64*
3.75	144*	120	112*	96*	90	80*	80*	72*
4.00	152*	128	120*	104*	96	88*	80*	72*
4.25	160*	144*	128*	112*	104*	96*	88*	80*
4.50	168*	152*	136*	120*	112*	96*	96*	88*
4.75	176*	160*	144*	128*	114	104*	96*	88*
5.00	192*	168*	144*	136*	120	112*	104*	96*

45 " WIDE FABRIC

TEMPLATE CODES

YARDS	R113	R114	R115	R116	R117	R118	R119	R120
0.25	12	10	8	8	6	6	6	6
0.50	24	20	16	16	12	12	12	12
0.75	36	30	24	24	20*	20*	20*	18
1.00	48	40	32	32	30*	24	24	24
1.25	60	50	40	40	30	30	30	30
1.50	72	60	50*	50*	40*	40*	40*	36
1.75	84	70	60*	60*	50*	50*	42	42
2.00	96	80	70*	64	60*	50*	50*	48
2.25	108	90	80*	72	70*	60*	60*	54
2.50	120	100	90*	80	70*	70*	60	60
2.75	132	110	100*	90*	80*	70*	70*	66
3.00	144	120	110*	100*	90*	80*	80*	72
3.25	156	130	120*	110*	100*	90*	80*	80*
3.50	168	140	130*	120*	100*	100*	90*	84
3.75	180	150	140*	120	110*	100*	100*	90
4.00	192	160	150*	130*	120*	110*	100*	96
4.25	204	180*	160*	140*	130*	120*	110*	102
4.50	216	190*	170*	150*	140*	120*	120*	110*
4.75	228	200*	180*	160*	140*	130*	120*	114
5.00	240	210*	180*	170*	150*	140*	130*	120

36 " WIDE FABRIC

TEMPLATE CODES

YARDS	R121	R122	R123	R124	R125	R126	R127	R128
0.25	4	4	4	2	2	2	2	2
0.50	8	8	8	4	4	4	4	4
0.75	12	12	12	8*	8*	8*	8*	8*
1.00	16	16	16	8	8	8	8	8
1.25	20	20	20	16*	16*	16*	16*	16*
1.50	24	24	24	16*	16*	16*	16*	16*
1.75	32*	28	28	24*	24*	24*	16*	16*
2.00	32	32	32	24*	24*	24*	24*	24*
2.25	40*	36	36	32*	32*	24*	24*	24*
2.50	40	40	40	32*	32*	32*	32*	32*
2.75	48*	48*	44	40*	40*	32*	32*	32*
3.00	48	48	48	40*	40*	40*	40*	32*
3.25	56*	56*	52	48*	48*	40*	40*	40*
3.50	64*	56	56	48*	48*	48*	40*	40*
3.75	64*	64*	60	56*	48*	48*	48*	48*
4.00	72*	64	64	56*	56*	56*	48*	48*
4.25	72*	72*	68	64*	56*	56*	56*	48*
4.50	80*	72	72	64*	64*	56*	56*	56*
4.75	88*	80*	76	72*	64*	64*	56*	56*
5.00	88*	80	80	72*	72*	64*	64*	64*

45 " WIDE FABRIC

TEMPLATE CODES

YARDS	R121	R122	R123	R124	R125	R126	R127	R128
0.25	4	4	4	4	4	4	4	4
0.50	10*	10*	10*	8	8	8	8	8
0.75	12	12	12	12	12	12	12	12
1.00	20*	20*	20*	16	16	16	16	16
1.25	20	20	20	20	20	20	20	20
1.50	30*	30*	30*	24	24	24	24	24
1.75	40*	30*	30*	30*	30*	30*	28	28
2.00	40*	40*	40*	32	32	32	32	32
2.25	50*	40*	40*	40*	40*	36	36	36
2.50	50*	50*	50*	40	40	40	40	40
2.75	60*	60*	50*	50*	50*	44	44	44
3.00	60*	60*	60*	50*	50*	50*	50*	48
3.25	70*	70*	60*	60*	60*	52	52	52
3.50	80*	70*	70*	60*	60*	60*	56	56
3.75	80*	80*	70*	70*	60	60	60	60
4.00	90*	80*	80*	70*	70*	70*	64	64
4.25	90*	90*	80*	80*	70*	70*	70*	68
4.50	100*	90*	90*	80*	80*	72	72	72
4.75	110*	100*	90*	90*	80*	80*	76	76
5.00	110*	100*	100*	90*	90*	80	80	80

36 " WIDE FABRIC

TEMPLATE CODES

YARDS	R129	R130	R131	R132	R133	R134	R135	R136
0.25	2	2	2	7*	7*	7*	3	3
0.50	4	4	4	15	14*	14*	9	9
0.75	8*	8*	8*	25	21*	21*	15	15
1.00	8	8	8	35	28	28	21	21
1.25	10	10	10	45	36	36	28*	28*
1.50	16*	16*	16*	50	42*	42*	35*	30
1.75	16*	16*	16*	63*	49*	49*	42*	36
2.00	24*	16	16	70	63*	56	49*	42
2.25	24*	24*	24*	80	70*	64	56*	49*
2.50	24*	24*	24*	90	77*	72	63*	56*
2.75	32*	32*	24*	98*	84*	77*	63*	63*
3.00	32*	32*	32*	105	91*	84	70*	63
3.25	32*	32*	32*	115	98*	92	77*	70*
3.50	40*	40*	32*	126*	105*	100	84*	77*
3.75	40*	40*	40*	135	112*	108	91*	84*
4.00	48*	40*	40*	140	126*	112	98*	91*
4.25	48*	48*	48*	150	133*	120	105*	91*
4.50	48*	48*	48*	161*	140*	128	112*	98*
4.75	56*	48*	48*	170	147*	136	119*	105*
5.00	56*	56*	56*	180	154*	144	126*	112*

45 " WIDE FABRIC

TEMPLATE CODES

YARDS	R129	R130	R131	R132	R133	R134	R135	R136
0.25	2	2	2	9*	9*	9*	4	4
0.50	4	4	4	18	18*	18*	12	12
0.75	10*	10*	10*	30	27*	27*	20	20
1.00	10*	10*	10*	45*	36*	36*	28	28
1.25	10	10	10	54	45	45	36	36
1.50	20*	20*	20*	63*	54*	54*	45*	40
1.75	20*	20*	20*	81*	63*	63*	54*	48
2.00	30*	20*	20*	90*	81*	72*	63*	56
2.25	30*	30*	30*	99*	90*	81*	72*	64
2.50	30*	30*	30*	108	99*	90	81*	72
2.75	40*	40*	30*	126*	108*	99*	81*	81*
3.00	40*	40*	40*	135*	117*	108*	90*	84
3.25	40*	40*	40*	144*	126*	117*	99*	92
3.50	50*	50*	40*	162*	135*	126*	108*	100
3.75	50*	50*	50*	171*	144*	135	117*	108
4.00	60*	50*	50*	180*	162*	144*	126*	117*
4.25	60*	60*	60*	189*	171*	153*	135*	120
4.50	60*	60*	60*	207*	180*	162*	144*	128
4.75	70*	60*	60*	216*	189*	171*	153*	136
5.00	70*	70*	70*	225*	198*	180	162*	144

36 " WIDE FABRIC

TEMPLATE CODES

YARDS	R137	R138	R139	R140	R141	R142	R143	R144
0.25	3	2	2	2	2	2	2	1
0.50	9	7*	7*	7*	7*	7*	7*	3
0.75	15	14*	10	10	10	10	10	7*
1.00	21	14	14	14	14	14	14	7
1.25	27	21*	21*	21*	18	18	18	14*
1.50	30	28*	21*	21*	21*	21*	21*	14*
1.75	36	28*	28*	28*	24	24	24	21*
2.00	42	35*	35*	28	28	28	28	21*
2.25	48	42*	35*	35*	35*	32	32	28*
2.50	54	42*	42*	42*	36	36	36	28*
2.75	57	49*	49*	42*	42*	38	38	35*
3.00	63	56*	49*	49*	42	42	42	35*
3.25	69	63*	56*	49*	49*	46	46	42*
3.50	75	63*	63*	56*	50	50	50	42*
3.75	81	70*	63*	63*	56*	54	54	49*
4.00	84	77*	70*	63*	63*	56	56	49*
4.25	90	77*	70*	70*	63*	63*	60	56*
4.50	96	84*	77*	70*	70*	64	64	56*
4.75	102	91*	84*	77*	70*	70*	68	63*
5.00	108	91*	84*	84*	77*	72	72	63*

45 " WIDE FABRIC

TEMPLATE CODES

YARDS	R137	R138	R139	R140	R141	R142	R143	R144
0.25	3	3	3	3	2	2	2	2
0.50	9	9	9	9	9*	9*	9*	6
0.75	18*	18*	15	15	10	10	10	10
1.00	27*	21	21	21	18*	18*	18*	14
1.25	27	27	27	27	18	18	18	18
1.50	36*	36*	30	30	27*	27*	27*	20
1.75	45*	36	36	36	27*	27*	27*	27*
2.00	54*	45*	45*	42	36*	36*	36*	28
2.25	54*	54*	48	48	45*	36*	36*	36*
2.50	63*	54	54	54	45*	45*	45*	36
2.75	72*	63*	63*	57	54*	45*	45*	45*
3.00	81*	72*	63	63	54*	54*	54*	45*
3.25	81*	81*	72*	69	63*	54*	54*	54*
3.50	90*	81*	81*	75	63*	63*	63*	54*
3.75	99*	90*	81	81	72*	63*	63*	63*
4.00	108*	99*	90*	84	81*	72*	72*	63*
4.25	108*	99*	90	90	81*	81*	72*	72*
4.50	117*	108*	99*	96	90*	81*	81*	72*
4.75	126*	117*	108*	102	90*	90*	81*	81*
5.00	135*	117*	108	108	99*	90*	90*	81*

36 " WIDE FABRIC

TEMPLATE CODES

YARDS	R145	R146	R147	R148	R149	R150	R151	R152
0.25	1	1	1	1	1	1	1	6*
0.50	3	3	3	3	3	3	3	12
0.75	7*	7*	7*	7*	7*	7*	7*	18*
1.00	7	7	7	7	7	7	7	24
1.25	14*	14*	14*	9	9	9	9	36*
1.50	14*	14*	14*	14*	14*	14*	14*	42*
1.75	21*	21*	14*	14*	14*	14*	14*	48*
2.00	21*	21*	21*	21*	21*	14	14	54*
2.25	28*	21*	21*	21*	21*	21*	21*	60*
2.50	28*	28*	28*	21*	21*	21*	21*	72*
2.75	28*	28*	28*	28*	28*	21*	21*	78*
3.00	35*	35*	28*	28*	28*	28*	28*	84*
3.25	35*	35*	35*	35*	28*	28*	28*	90*
3.50	42*	42*	35*	35*	35*	35*	28*	96*
3.75	42*	42*	42*	35*	35*	35*	35*	108*
4.00	49*	42*	42*	42*	42*	35*	35*	114*
4.25	49*	49*	42*	42*	42*	42*	35*	120*
4.50	56*	49*	49*	49*	42*	42*	42*	126*
4.75	56*	56*	49*	49*	49*	42*	42*	132*
5.00	63*	56*	56*	49*	49*	49*	42*	144*

45 " WIDE FABRIC

TEMPLATE CODES

YARDS	R145	R146	R147	R148	R149	R150	R151	R152
0.25	2	2	2	1	1	1	1	8*
0.50	6	6	6	3	3	3	3	18
0.75	10	10	10	9*	9*	9*	9*	24
1.00	14	14	14	9*	9*	9*	9*	36
1.25	18	18	18	9	9	9	9	48
1.50	20	20	20	18*	18*	18*	18*	56*
1.75	27*	27*	24	18*	18*	18*	18*	66
2.00	28	28	28	27*	27*	18*	18*	78
2.25	36*	32	32	27*	27*	27*	27*	84
2.50	36	36	36	27*	27*	27*	27*	96
2.75	38	38	38	36*	36*	27*	27*	108
3.00	45*	45*	42	36*	36*	36*	36*	114
3.25	46	46	46	45*	36*	36*	36*	126
3.50	54*	54*	50	45*	45*	45*	36*	132
3.75	54	54	54	45*	45*	45*	45*	144
4.00	63*	56	56	54*	54*	45*	45*	156
4.25	63*	63*	60	54*	54*	54*	45*	162
4.50	72*	64	64	63*	54*	54*	54*	174
4.75	72*	72*	68	63*	63*	54*	54*	186
5.00	81*	72	72	63*	63*	63*	54*	192

36 " WIDE FABRIC

TEMPLATE CODES

YARDS	R153	R154	R155	R156	R157	R158	R159	R160
0.25	6*	3	3	3	2	2	2	2
0.50	12	9	9	9	6	6	6	6
0.75	18*	12	12	12	12*	12*	8	8
1.00	24	18	18	18	12	12	12	12
1.25	32	24	24	24	18*	18*	18*	16
1.50	36	30*	30*	27	24*	24*	18	18
1.75	44	36*	36*	33	30*	24*	24*	24*
2.00	52	42*	39	39	30*	30*	26	26
2.25	56	48*	42	42	36*	36*	30*	30*
2.50	64	54*	48	48	42*	36*	36*	32
2.75	72	60*	54	54	42*	42*	36	36
3.00	76	66*	60*	57	48*	48*	42*	38
3.25	84	72*	66*	63	54*	48*	48*	42
3.50	88	78*	72*	66	60*	54*	48*	48*
3.75	96	84*	72	72	60*	60*	54*	48
4.00	104	90*	78	78	66*	60*	54*	54*
4.25	108	96*	84*	81	72*	66*	60*	54
4.50	116	102*	90*	87	72*	72*	66*	60*
4.75	124	108*	96*	93	78*	72*	66*	66*
5.00	128	108*	102*	96	84*	78*	72*	66*

45 " WIDE FABRIC

TEMPLATE CODES

YARDS	R153	R154	R155	R156	R157	R158	R159	R160
0.25	8*	4	4	3	3	3	3	2
0.50	16*	12	12	9	9	9	9	8*
0.75	24*	16	16	16*	16*	16*	12	8
1.00	32*	24	24	24*	18	18	18	16*
1.25	40	32	32	24	24	24	24	16
1.50	48*	40*	40*	32*	32*	32*	27	24*
1.75	56*	48*	48*	40*	40*	33	33	32*
2.00	65	56*	52	48*	40*	40*	39	32*
2.25	72*	64*	56	56*	48*	48*	42	40*
2.50	80	72*	64	56*	56*	48	48	40*
2.75	90	80*	72	64*	56*	56*	54	48*
3.00	96*	88*	80*	72*	64*	64*	57	48*
3.25	105	96*	88*	80*	72*	64*	64*	56*
3.50	112*	104*	96*	80*	80*	72*	66	64*
3.75	120	112*	96	88*	80*	80*	72	64*
4.00	130	120*	104	96*	88*	80*	78	72*
4.25	144*	128*	112*	104*	96*	88*	81	72*
4.50	152*	136*	120*	112*	96*	96*	88*	80*
4.75	160*	144*	128*	112*	104*	96*	93	88*
5.00	168*	144*	136*	120*	112*	104*	96	88*

36 " WIDE FABRIC

TEMPLATE CODES

YARDS	R161	R162	R163	R164	R165	R166	R167	R168
0.25	2	2	1	1	1	1	1	1
0.50	6	6	3	3	3	3	3	3
0.75	8	8	6*	6*	6*	6*	6*	6*
1.00	12	12	6	6	6	6	6	6
1.25	16	16	12*	12*	12*	12*	12*	8
1.50	18	18	12*	12*	12*	12*	12*	12*
1.75	22	22	18*	18*	18*	12*	12*	12*
2.00	26	26	18*	18*	18*	18*	18*	18*
2.25	28	28	24*	24*	18*	18*	18*	18*
2.50	32	32	24*	24*	24*	24*	24*	18*
2.75	36	36	30*	30*	24*	24*	24*	24*
3.00	38	38	30*	30*	30*	30*	24*	24*
3.25	42	42	36*	36*	30*	30*	30*	24*
3.50	44	44	36*	36*	36*	30*	30*	30*
3.75	48	48	42*	36*	36*	36*	36*	30*
4.00	52	52	42*	42*	42*	36*	36*	36*
4.25	54	54	48*	42*	42*	42*	36*	36*
4.50	58	58	48*	48*	42*	42*	42*	36*
4.75	62	62	54*	48*	48*	42*	42*	42*
5.00	64	64	54*	54*	48*	48*	48*	42*

45 " WIDE FABRIC

TEMPLATE CODES

YARDS	R161	R162	R163	R164	R165	R166	R167	R168
0.25	2	2	2	2	2	2	2	1
0.50	8*	8*	6	6	6	6	6	3
0.75	8	8	8	8	8	8	8	8*
1.00	16*	16*	12	12	12	12	12	8*
1.25	16	16	16	16	16	16	16	8
1.50	24*	24*	18	18	18	18	18	16*
1.75	24*	24*	24*	24*	24*	22	22	16*
2.00	32*	32*	26	26	26	26	26	24*
2.25	32*	32*	32*	32*	28	28	28	24*
2.50	40*	40*	32	32	32	32	32	24*
2.75	48*	40*	40*	40*	36	36	36	32*
3.00	48*	48*	40*	40*	40*	40*	38	32*
3.25	56*	48*	48*	48*	42	42	42	32*
3.50	56*	56*	48*	48*	48*	44	44	40*
3.75	64*	56*	56*	48	48	48	48	40*
4.00	64*	64*	56*	56*	56*	52	52	48*
4.25	72*	64*	64*	56*	56*	56*	54	48*
4.50	72*	72*	64*	64*	58	58	58	48*
4.75	80*	72*	72*	64*	64*	62	62	56*
5.00	80*	80*	72*	72*	64	64	64	56*

36 " WIDE FABRIC

TEMPLATE CODES

YARDS	R169	R170	R171	R172	R173	R174	R175	R176
0.25	1	1	6*	6*	3	3	3	2
0.50	3	3	12	12	9	9	9	6
0.75	6*	6*	18*	18*	12	12	12	12*
1.00	6	6	24	24	18	18	18	12
1.25	8	8	30*	30*	24*	24*	21	18*
1.50	12*	12*	36	36	30*	27	27	24*
1.75	12*	12*	42*	42*	36*	30	30	24*
2.00	13	13	54*	48	42*	36	36	30*
2.25	18*	18*	60*	54*	48*	42*	39	36*
2.50	18*	18*	66*	60	54*	48*	45	36*
2.75	24*	18	72*	66*	54*	54*	48	42*
3.00	24*	24*	78*	72	60*	54	54	48*
3.25	24*	24*	84*	78*	66*	60*	57	54*
3.50	30*	24*	90*	84	72*	66*	63	54*
3.75	30*	30*	96*	90*	78*	72*	66	60*
4.00	30*	30*	108*	96	84*	78*	72	66*
4.25	36*	36*	114*	102*	90*	78*	75	66*
4.50	36*	36*	120*	108	96*	84*	81	72*
4.75	36*	36*	126*	114*	102*	90*	84	78*
5.00	42*	42*	132*	120	108*	96*	90	78*

45 " WIDE FABRIC

TEMPLATE CODES

YARDS	R169	R170	R171	R172	R173	R174	R175	R176
0.25	1	1	7*	7*	4	4	3	3
0.50	3	3	15	15	12	12	9	9
0.75	8*	8*	21*	21*	16	16	14*	14*
1.00	8*	8*	30	30	24	24	21*	18
1.25	8	8	35	35	28	28	21	21
1.50	16*	16*	45	45	36	36	28*	28*
1.75	16*	16*	50	50	42*	40	35*	30
2.00	16*	16*	63*	60	49*	48	42*	36
2.25	24*	24*	70*	65	56*	52	42*	42*
2.50	24*	24*	77*	75	63*	60	49*	45
2.75	32*	24*	84*	80	64	64	56*	49*
3.00	32*	32*	91*	90	72	72	63*	56*
3.25	32*	32*	98*	95	77*	76	63*	63*
3.50	40*	32*	105	105	84	84	70*	63
3.75	40*	40*	112*	110	91*	88	77*	70*
4.00	40*	40*	126*	120	98*	96	84*	77*
4.25	48*	48*	133*	125	105*	100	84*	77*
4.50	48*	48*	140*	135	112*	108	91*	84*
4.75	48*	48*	147*	140	119*	112	98*	91*
5.00	56*	56*	154*	150	126*	120	105*	91*

36 " WIDE FABRIC

TEMPLATE CODES

YARDS	R177	R178	R179	R180	R181	R182	R183	R184
0.25	2	2	2	2	2	1	1	1
0.50	6	6	6	6	6	3	3	3
0.75	8	8	8	8	8	6*	6*	6*
1.00	12	12	12	12	12	6	6	6
1.25	18*	18*	14	14	14	12*	12*	12*
1.50	18	18	18	18	18	12*	12*	12*
1.75	24*	24*	20	20	20	18*	18*	18*
2.00	30*	24	24	24	24	18*	18*	18*
2.25	30*	30*	30*	26	26	24*	24*	18*
2.50	36*	36*	30	30	30	24*	24*	24*
2.75	42*	36*	36*	32	32	30*	24*	24*
3.00	42*	42*	36	36	36	30*	30*	30*
3.25	48*	42*	42*	38	38	36*	30*	30*
3.50	54*	48*	42	42	42	36*	36*	36*
3.75	54*	54*	48*	44	44	42*	36*	36*
4.00	60*	54*	54*	48	48	42*	42*	36*
4.25	60*	60*	54*	54*	50	48*	42*	42*
4.50	66*	60*	60*	54	54	48*	48*	42*
4.75	72*	66*	60*	60*	56	54*	48*	48*
5.00	72*	72*	66*	60	60	54*	54*	48*

45 " WIDE FABRIC

TEMPLATE CODES

YARDS	R177	R178	R179	R180	R181	R182	R183	R184
0.25	3	3	2	2	2	2	2	2
0.50	9	9	7*	7*	7*	6	6	6
0.75	12	12	8	8	8	8	8	8
1.00	18	18	14*	14*	14*	12	12	12
1.25	21	21	14	14	14	14	14	14
1.50	27	27	21*	21*	21*	18	18	18
1.75	30	30	21*	21*	21*	21*	21*	21*
2.00	36	36	28*	28*	28*	24	24	24
2.25	39	39	35*	28*	28*	28*	28*	26
2.50	45	45	35*	35*	35*	30	30	30
2.75	49*	48	42*	35*	35*	35*	32	32
3.00	54	54	42*	42*	42*	36	36	36
3.25	57	57	49*	42*	42*	42*	38	38
3.50	63	63	49*	49*	49*	42	42	42
3.75	66	66	56*	49*	49*	49*	44	44
4.00	72	72	63*	56*	56*	49*	49*	48
4.25	75	75	63*	63*	56*	56*	50	50
4.50	81	81	70*	63*	63*	56*	56*	54
4.75	84	84	70*	70*	63*	63*	56	56
5.00	90	90	77*	70*	70*	63*	63*	60

36 " WIDE FABRIC

TEMPLATE CODES

YARDS	R185	R186	R187	R188	R189	R190	R191	R192
0.25	1	1	1	1	1	5*	3	3
0.50	3	3	3	3	3	10*	6	6
0.75	6*	6*	6*	6*	6*	16	12	12
1.00	6	6	6	6	6	20	15	15
1.25	12*	7	7	7	7	25*	20*	20*
1.50	12*	12*	12*	12*	12*	32	25*	25*
1.75	12*	12*	12*	12*	12*	36	30*	30*
2.00	18*	18*	18*	12	12	44	35*	33
2.25	18*	18*	18*	18*	18*	48	40*	36
2.50	24*	18*	18*	18*	18*	52	45*	40*
2.75	24*	24*	24*	18*	18*	60	50*	45
3.00	24*	24*	24*	24*	24*	64	55*	50*
3.25	30*	30*	24*	24*	24*	72	60*	55*
3.50	30*	30*	30*	30*	24*	76	65*	60*
3.75	36*	30*	30*	30*	30*	80	70*	60
4.00	36*	36*	36*	30*	30*	88	75*	66
4.25	36*	36*	36*	36*	30*	92	80*	70*
4.50	42*	42*	36*	36*	36*	96	85*	75*
4.75	42*	42*	42*	36*	36*	104	90*	80*
5.00	48*	42*	42*	42*	36*	108	90*	85*

45 " WIDE FABRIC

TEMPLATE CODES

YARDS	R185	R186	R187	R188	R189	R190	R191	R192
0.25	2	1	1	1	1	6*	4	4
0.50	6	3	3	3	3	12*	8	8
0.75	8	7*	7*	7*	7*	20	16	16
1.00	12	7*	7*	7*	7*	25	20	20
1.25	14	7	7	7	7	30	24	24
1.50	18	14*	14*	14*	14*	40	32	32
1.75	20	14*	14*	14*	14*	45	36	36
2.00	24	21*	21*	14*	14*	55	44	44
2.25	26	21*	21*	21*	21*	60	48	48
2.50	30	21*	21*	21*	21*	65	54*	52
2.75	32	28*	28*	21*	21*	75	60	60
3.00	36	28*	28*	28*	28*	80	66*	64
3.25	38	35*	28*	28*	28*	90	72	72
3.50	42	35*	35*	35*	28*	95	78*	76
3.75	44	35*	35*	35*	35*	100	84*	80
4.00	48	42*	42*	35*	35*	110	90*	88
4.25	50	42*	42*	42*	35*	115	96*	92
4.50	54	49*	42*	42*	42*	120	102*	96
4.75	56	49*	49*	42*	42*	130	108*	104
5.00	60	49*	49*	49*	42*	135	108	108

36 " WIDE FABRIC

TEMPLATE CODES

YARDS	R193	R194	R195	R196	R197	R198	R199	R200
0.25	3	2	2	2	2	2	2	1
0.50	6	5*	5*	5*	5*	5*	5*	2
0.75	12	10*	10*	8	8	8	8	5*
1.00	15	10	10	10	10	10	10	5
1.25	18	15*	15*	15*	12	12	12	10*
1.50	24	20*	20*	16	16	16	16	10*
1.75	27	25*	20*	20*	20*	18	18	15*
2.00	33	25*	25*	22	22	22	22	15*
2.25	36	30*	30*	25*	25*	24	24	20*
2.50	39	35*	30*	30*	26	26	26	20*
2.75	45	35*	35*	30	30	30	30	25*
3.00	48	40*	40*	35*	32	32	32	25*
3.25	54	45*	40*	40*	36	36	36	30*
3.50	57	50*	45*	40*	40*	38	38	30*
3.75	60	50*	50*	45*	40	40	40	35*
4.00	66	55*	50*	45*	45*	44	44	35*
4.25	69	60*	55*	50*	46	46	46	40*
4.50	72	60*	60*	55*	50*	48	48	40*
4.75	78	65*	60*	55*	55*	52	52	45*
5.00	81	70*	65*	60*	55*	54	54	45*

45 " WIDE FABRIC

TEMPLATE CODES

YARDS	R193	R194	R195	R196	R197	R198	R199	R200
0.25	3	3	3	3	2	2	2	2
0.50	6	6	6	6	6*	6*	6*	4
0.75	12	12	12	12	8	8	8	8
1.00	18*	15	15	15	12*	12*	12*	10
1.25	18	18	18	18	12	12	12	12
1.50	24	24	24	24	18*	18*	18*	16
1.75	30*	30*	27	27	24*	18	18	18
2.00	36*	33	33	33	24*	24*	24*	22
2.25	42*	36	36	36	30*	24	24	24
2.50	42*	42*	39	39	30*	30*	30*	26
2.75	48*	45	45	45	36*	36*	30	30
3.00	54*	48	48	48	36*	36*	36*	32
3.25	60*	54	54	54	42*	42*	36	36
3.50	60*	60*	57	57	48*	42*	42*	38
3.75	66*	60	60	60	48*	48*	42*	42*
4.00	72*	66	66	66	54*	48*	48*	44
4.25	78*	72*	69	69	54*	54*	48*	48*
4.50	84*	72	72	72	60*	54*	54*	48
4.75	84*	78	78	78	66*	60*	54*	54*
5.00	90*	84*	81	81	66*	60*	60*	54

36 " WIDE FABRIC

TEMPLATE CODES

YARDS	R201	R202	R203	R204	R205	R206	R207	R208
0.25	1	1	1	1	1	1	1	5*
0.50	2	2	2	2	2	2	2	10*
0.75	5*	5*	5*	5*	5*	5*	5*	15*
1.00	5	5	5	5	5	5	5	20
1.25	10*	10*	10*	10*	6	6	6	25*
1.50	10*	10*	10*	10*	10*	10*	10*	30*
1.75	15*	15*	10*	10*	10*	10*	10*	36
2.00	15*	15*	15*	15*	15*	11	11	40
2.25	20*	15*	15*	15*	15*	15*	15*	45*
2.50	20*	20*	20*	20*	15*	15*	15*	50*
2.75	25*	20*	20*	20*	20*	20*	15	56
3.00	25*	25*	25*	20*	20*	20*	20*	60
3.25	30*	25*	25*	25*	20*	20*	20*	65*
3.50	30*	30*	25*	25*	25*	25*	20*	72
3.75	30*	30*	30*	30*	25*	25*	25*	76
4.00	35*	35*	30*	30*	30*	25*	25*	80
4.25	35*	35*	35*	30*	30*	30*	30*	85*
4.50	40*	35*	35*	35*	30*	30*	30*	92
4.75	40*	40*	35*	35*	35*	30*	30*	96
5.00	45*	40*	40*	40*	35*	35*	35*	100

45 " WIDE FABRIC

TEMPLATE CODES

YARDS	R201	R202	R203	R204	R205	R206	R207	R208
0.25	2	2	2	2	1	1	1	6*
0.50	4	4	4	4	2	2	2	12*
0.75	8	8	8	8	6*	6*	6*	18*
1.00	10	10	10	10	6*	6*	6*	25
1.25	12	12	12	12	6	6	6	30
1.50	16	16	16	16	12*	12*	12*	36*
1.75	18	18	18	18	12*	12*	12*	45
2.00	22	22	22	22	18*	12*	12*	50
2.25	24	24	24	24	18*	18*	18*	55
2.50	26	26	26	26	18*	18*	18*	60
2.75	30	30	30	30	24*	24*	18*	70
3.00	32	32	32	32	24*	24*	24*	75
3.25	36	36	36	36	24*	24*	24*	80
3.50	38	38	38	38	30*	30*	24*	90
3.75	40	40	40	40	30*	30*	30*	95
4.00	44	44	44	44	36*	30*	30*	100
4.25	46	46	46	46	36*	36*	36*	105
4.50	48	48	48	48	36*	36*	36*	115
4.75	52	52	52	52	42*	36*	36*	120
5.00	54	54	54	54	42*	42*	42*	125

36 " WIDE FABRIC

TEMPLATE CODES

YARDS	R209	R210	R211	R212	R213	R214	R215	R216
0.25	3	3	3	2	2	2	2	2
0.50	6	6	6	5*	5*	5*	5*	5*
0.75	10*	10*	10*	10*	6	6	6	6
1.00	15	15	15	10	10	10	10	10
1.25	20*	20*	18	15*	15*	15*	12	12
1.50	25*	21	21	20*	15*	15*	15*	15*
1.75	30*	27	27	20*	20*	20*	18	18
2.00	35*	30	30	25*	25*	20	20	20
2.25	40*	35*	33	30*	25*	25*	25*	22
2.50	45*	40*	36	30*	30*	30*	25*	25*
2.75	45*	45*	42	35*	35*	30*	30*	28
3.00	50*	45	45	40*	35*	35*	30	30
3.25	55*	50*	48	45*	40*	35*	35*	32
3.50	60*	55*	54	45*	45*	40*	36	36
3.75	65*	60*	57	50*	45*	45*	40*	38
4.00	70*	65*	60	55*	50*	45*	45*	40
4.25	75*	65*	63	55*	50*	50*	45*	45*
4.50	80*	70*	69	60*	55*	50*	50*	46
4.75	85*	75*	72	65*	60*	55*	50*	50*
5.00	90*	80*	75	65*	60*	60*	55*	50

45 " WIDE FABRIC

TEMPLATE CODES

YARDS	R209	R210	R211	R212	R213	R214	R215	R216
0.25	4	4	3	3	3	3	2	2
0.50	8	8	6	6	6	6	6*	6*
0.75	12	12	12*	12*	9	9	6	6
1.00	20	20	18*	15	15	15	12*	12*
1.25	24	24	18	18	18	18	12	12
1.50	30*	28	24*	24*	21	21	18*	18*
1.75	36	36	30*	27	27	27	18	18
2.00	42*	40	36*	30	30	30	24*	24*
2.25	48*	44	36*	36*	33	33	30*	24*
2.50	54*	48	42*	36	36	36	30*	30*
2.75	56	56	48*	42	42	42	36*	30*
3.00	60	60	54*	48*	45	45	36*	36*
3.25	66*	64	54*	54*	48	48	42*	36*
3.50	72	72	60*	54	54	54	42*	42*
3.75	78*	76	66*	60*	57	57	48*	42*
4.00	84*	80	72*	66*	60	60	54*	48*
4.25	90*	84	72*	66*	63	63	54*	54*
4.50	96*	92	78*	72*	69	69	60*	54*
4.75	102*	96	84*	78*	72	72	60*	60*
5.00	108*	100	90*	78*	75	75	66*	60*

36 " WIDE FABRIC

TEMPLATE CODES

YARDS	R217	R218	R219	R220	R221	R222	R223	R224
0.25	2	1	1	1	1	1	1	1
0.50	5*	2	2	2	2	2	2	2
0.75	6	5*	5*	5*	5*	5*	5*	5*
1.00	10	5	5	5	5	5	5	5
1.25	12	10*	10*	10*	10*	6	6	6
1.50	15*	10*	10*	10*	10*	10*	10*	10*
1.75	18	15*	15*	15*	10*	10*	10*	10*
2.00	20	15*	15*	15*	15*	15*	15*	10
2.25	22	20*	20*	15*	15*	15*	15*	15*
2.50	25*	20*	20*	20*	20*	15*	15*	15*
2.75	28	25*	20*	20*	20*	20*	20*	15*
3.00	30	25*	25*	25*	20*	20*	20*	20*
3.25	32	30*	25*	25*	25*	25*	20*	20*
3.50	36	30*	30*	30*	25*	25*	25*	25*
3.75	38	35*	30*	30*	30*	25*	25*	25*
4.00	40	35*	35*	30*	30*	30*	30*	25*
4.25	42	40*	35*	35*	30*	30*	30*	30*
4.50	46	40*	40*	35*	35*	35*	30*	30*
4.75	48	45*	40*	40*	35*	35*	35*	30*
5.00	50	45*	45*	40*	40*	35*	35*	35*

45 " WIDE FABRIC

TEMPLATE CODES

YARDS	R217	R218	R219	R220	R221	R222	R223	R224
0.25	2	2	2	2	2	1	1	1
0.50	6*	4	4	4	4	2	2	2
0.75	6	6	6	6	6	6*	6*	6*
1.00	12*	10	10	10	10	6*	6*	6*
1.25	12	12	12	12	12	6	6	6
1.50	18*	14	14	14	14	12*	12*	12*
1.75	18	18	18	18	18	12*	12*	12*
2.00	24*	20	20	20	20	18*	18*	12*
2.25	24*	24*	24*	22	22	18*	18*	18*
2.50	30*	24	24	24	24	18*	18*	18*
2.75	30*	30*	28	28	28	24*	24*	18*
3.00	36*	30	30	30	30	24*	24*	24*
3.25	36*	36*	32	32	32	30*	24*	24*
3.50	42*	36	36	36	36	30*	30*	30*
3.75	42*	42*	38	38	38	30*	30*	30*
4.00	48*	42*	42*	40	40	36*	36*	30*
4.25	48*	48*	42	42	42	36*	36*	36*
4.50	54*	48*	48*	46	46	42*	36*	36*
4.75	54*	54*	48	48	48	42*	42*	36*
5.00	60*	54*	54*	50	50	42*	42*	42*

36 " WIDE FABRIC

TEMPLATE CODES

YARDS	R225	R226	R227	R228	R229	R230	R231	R232
0.25	1	3	3	3	2	2	2	2
0.50	2	6	6	6	4	4	4	4
0.75	5*	9	9	9	8*	8*	6	6
1.00	5	12	12	12	8	8	8	8
1.25	6	18	18	18	12	12	12	12
1.50	10*	21	21	21	16*	16*	14	14
1.75	10*	24	24	24	20*	16	16	16
2.00	10	28*	27	27	20*	20*	18	18
2.25	15*	32*	30	30	24*	24*	20	20
2.50	15*	36	36	36	28*	24	24	24
2.75	15*	40*	39	39	28*	28*	26	26
3.00	20*	44*	42	42	32*	32*	28	28
3.25	20*	48*	45	45	36*	32*	32*	30
3.50	20*	52*	48	48	40*	36*	32	32
3.75	25*	56*	54	54	40*	40*	36	36
4.00	25*	60*	57	57	44*	40*	38	38
4.25	25*	64*	60	60	48*	44*	40	40
4.50	30*	68*	63	63	48*	48*	44*	42
4.75	30*	72*	66	66	52*	48*	44	44
5.00	30*	72	72	72	56*	52*	48	48

45 " WIDE FABRIC

TEMPLATE CODES

YARDS	R225	R226	R227	R228	R229	R230	R231	R232
0.25	1	4	4	3	3	3	3	2
0.50	2	8	8	6	6	6	6	6*
0.75	6*	12	12	12*	12*	12*	9	6
1.00	6*	18*	18*	18*	12	12	12	12*
1.25	6	24	24	18	18	18	18	12
1.50	12*	30*	30*	24*	24*	24*	21	18*
1.75	12*	36*	36*	30*	30*	24	24	24*
2.00	12*	42*	36	36*	30*	30*	27	24*
2.25	18*	48*	42*	42*	36*	36*	30	30*
2.50	18*	54*	48	42*	42*	36	36	30*
2.75	18*	60*	54*	48*	42*	42*	39	36*
3.00	24*	66*	60*	54*	48*	48*	42	36*
3.25	24*	72*	66*	60*	54*	48*	48*	42*
3.50	24*	78*	72*	60*	60*	54*	48	48*
3.75	30*	84*	72	66*	60*	60*	54	48*
4.00	30*	90*	78*	72*	66*	60*	57	54*
4.25	30*	96*	84*	78*	72*	66*	60	54*
4.50	36*	102*	90*	84*	72*	72*	66*	60*
4.75	36*	108*	96*	84*	78*	72*	66	66*
5.00	36*	108*	102*	90*	84*	78*	72	66*

36 " WIDE FABRIC

TEMPLATE CODES

YARDS	R241	R242	R243	R244	R245	R246	R247	R248
0.25	1	1	3	3	3	2	2	2
0.50	2	2	6	6	6	4	4	4
0.75	4*	4*	9	9	9	8*	6	6
1.00	4	4	12	12	12	8	8	8
1.25	6	6	16*	16*	15	12*	12*	12*
1.50	8*	8*	20*	18	18	16*	12	12
1.75	8	8	24*	21	21	16*	16*	16*
2.00	9	9	28*	27	27	20*	20*	18
2.25	12*	12*	32*	30	30	24*	20	20
2.50	12	12	36*	33	33	24*	24*	24*
2.75	16*	13	36	36	36	28*	28*	24
3.00	16*	16*	40*	39	39	32*	28*	28*
3.25	16*	16*	44*	42	42	36*	32*	28
3.50	20*	16	48*	45	45	36*	36*	32*
3.75	20*	20*	52*	48	48	40*	36*	36*
4.00	20*	20*	56*	54	54	44*	40*	36
4.25	24*	24*	60*	57	57	44*	40*	40*
4.50	24*	24*	64*	60	60	48*	44*	40
4.75	24*	24*	68*	63	63	52*	48*	44*
5.00	28*	28*	72*	66	66	52*	48*	48*

45 " WIDE FABRIC

TEMPLATE CODES

YARDS	R241	R242	R243	R244	R245	R246	R247	R248
0.25	1	1	4	4	3	3	3	3
0.50	2	2	8	8	6	6	6	6
0.75	6*	6*	12	12	10*	10*	9	9
1.00	6*	6*	16	16	15*	12	12	12
1.25	6	6	20	20	15	15	15	15
1.50	12*	12*	25*	24	20*	20*	18	18
1.75	12*	12*	30*	28	25*	21	21	21
2.00	12*	12*	36	36	30*	27	27	27
2.25	18*	18*	40	40	30	30	30	30
2.50	18*	18*	45*	44	35*	33	33	33
2.75	24*	18*	48	48	40*	36	36	36
3.00	24*	24*	52	52	45*	40*	39	39
3.25	24*	24*	56	56	45*	45*	42	42
3.50	30*	24*	60	60	50*	45	45	45
3.75	30*	30*	65*	64	55*	50*	48	48
4.00	30*	30*	72	72	60*	55*	54	54
4.25	36*	36*	76	76	60*	57	57	57
4.50	36*	36*	80	80	65*	60	60	60
4.75	36*	36*	85*	84	70*	65*	63	63
5.00	42*	42*	90*	88	75*	66	66	66

36 " WIDE FABRIC

TEMPLATE CODES

YARDS	R249	R250	R251	R252	R253	R254	R255	R256
0.25	2	2	2	1	1	1	1	1
0.50	4	4	4	2	2	2	2	2
0.75	6	6	6	4*	4*	4*	4*	4*
1.00	8	8	8	4	4	4	4	4
1.25	10	10	10	8*	8*	8*	8*	5
1.50	12	12	12	8*	8*	8*	8*	8*
1.75	14	14	14	12*	12*	12*	8*	8*
2.00	18	18	18	12*	12*	12*	12*	12*
2.25	20	20	20	16*	16*	12*	12*	12*
2.50	22	22	22	16*	16*	16*	16*	12*
2.75	24	24	24	20*	16*	16*	16*	16*
3.00	26	26	26	20*	20*	20*	16*	16*
3.25	28	28	28	24*	20*	20*	20*	20*
3.50	30	30	30	24*	24*	24*	20*	20*
3.75	32	32	32	28*	24*	24*	24*	20*
4.00	36	36	36	28*	28*	24*	24*	20*
4.25	38	38	38	32*	28*	28*	24*	24*
4.50	40	40	40	32*	32*	28*	28*	28*
4.75	42	42	42	36*	32*	32*	28*	28*
5.00	44	44	44	36*	36*	32*	32*	28*

45 " WIDE FABRIC

TEMPLATE CODES

YARDS	R249	R250	R251	R252	R253	R254	R255	R256
0.25	2	2	2	2	2	2	2	1
0.50	5*	5*	5*	4	4	4	4	2
0.75	6	6	6	6	6	6	6	5*
1.00	10*	10*	10*	8	8	8	8	5*
1.25	10	10	10	10	10	10	10	5
1.50	15*	15*	15*	12	12	12	12	10*
1.75	15*	15*	15*	15*	15*	15*	14	10*
2.00	20*	20*	20*	18	18	18	18	15*
2.25	25*	20	20	20	20	20	20	15*
2.50	25*	25*	25*	22	22	22	22	15*
2.75	30*	25*	25*	25*	24	24	24	20*
3.00	30*	30*	30*	26	26	26	26	20*
3.25	35*	30*	30*	30*	28	28	28	25*
3.50	35*	35*	35*	30	30	30	30	25*
3.75	40*	35*	35*	35*	32	32	32	25*
4.00	45*	40*	40*	36	36	36	36	30*
4.25	45*	45*	40*	40*	38	38	38	30*
4.50	50*	45*	45*	40	40	40	40	35*
4.75	50*	50*	45*	45*	42	42	42	35*
5.00	55*	50*	50*	45*	45*	44	44	35*

36 " WIDE FABRIC

TEMPLATE CODES

YARDS	R257	R258	R259	R260	R261	R262	R263	R264
0.25	1	1	1	3	3	2	2	2
0.50	2	2	2	6	6	4	4	4
0.75	4*	4*	4*	9	9	8*	8*	6
1.00	4	4	4	12	12	8	8	8
1.25	5	5	5	16*	15	12*	12*	12*
1.50	8*	8*	8*	20*	18	16*	16*	12
1.75	8*	8*	8*	24*	21	20*	16*	16*
2.00	12*	9	9	24	24	20*	20*	16
2.25	12*	12*	12*	28*	28*	24*	24*	20*
2.50	12*	12*	12*	32*	30	28*	24*	24*
2.75	16*	12	12	36*	33	28*	28*	24*
3.00	16*	16*	16*	40*	36	32*	32*	28*
3.25	16*	16*	16*	44*	40*	36*	32*	32*
3.50	20*	20*	16*	48*	42	40*	36*	32*
3.75	20*	20*	20*	48*	45	40*	40*	36*
4.00	24*	20*	20*	52*	48	44*	40*	36*
4.25	24*	24*	20*	56*	54	48*	44*	40*
4.50	24*	24*	24*	60*	57	48*	48*	44*
4.75	28*	24*	24*	64*	60	52*	48*	44*
5.00	28*	28*	24*	68*	63	56*	52*	48*

45 " WIDE FABRIC

TEMPLATE CODES

YARDS	R257	R258	R259	R260	R261	R262	R263	R264
0.25	1	1	1	4	3	3	3	3
0.50	2	2	2	8	6	6	6	6
0.75	5*	5*	5*	12	10*	10*	10*	9
1.00	5*	5*	5*	16	15*	12	12	12
1.25	5	5	5	20	15	15	15	15
1.50	10*	10*	10*	25*	20*	20*	20*	18
1.75	10*	10*	10*	30*	25*	25*	21	21
2.00	15*	10*	10*	32	30*	25*	25*	24
2.25	15*	15*	15*	36	35*	30*	30*	27
2.50	15*	15*	15*	40	35*	35*	30	30
2.75	20*	15*	15*	45*	40*	35*	35*	33
3.00	20*	20*	20*	50*	45*	40*	40*	36
3.25	20*	20*	20*	55*	50*	45*	40*	40*
3.50	25*	25*	20*	60*	50*	50*	45*	42
3.75	25*	25*	25*	60	55*	50*	50*	45
4.00	30*	25*	25*	65*	60*	55*	50*	48
4.25	30*	30*	25*	72	65*	60*	55*	54
4.50	30*	30*	30*	76	70*	60*	60*	57
4.75	35*	30*	30*	80	70*	65*	60	60
5.00	35*	35*	30*	85*	75*	70*	65*	63

36 " WIDE FABRIC

TEMPLATE CODES

YARDS	R265	R266	R267	R268	R269	R270	R271	R272
0.25	2	2	2	1	1	1	1	1
0.50	4	4	4	2	2	2	2	1
0.75	6	6	6	4*	4*	4*	4*	4*
1.00	8	8	8	4	4	4	4	4
1.25	10	10	10	8*	8*	8*	8*	8*
1.50	12	12	12	8*	8*	8*	8*	8*
1.75	16*	14	14	12*	12*	12*	8*	8*
2.00	16	16	16	12*	12*	12*	12*	12*
2.25	20*	18	18	16*	16*	12*	12*	12*
2.50	20	20	20	16*	16*	12*	12*	12*
2.75	24*	24*	22	20*	20*	16*	16*	16*
3.00	24	24	24	20*	20*	20*	20*	16*
3.25	28*	28*	26	24*	24*	20*	20*	20*
3.50	32*	28	28	24*	24*	24*	20*	20*
3.75	32*	32*	30	28*	24*	24*	24*	24*
4.00	36*	32	32	28*	28*	28*	24*	24*
4.25	36	36	36	32*	28*	28*	24*	24*
4.50	40*	38	38	32*	32*	28*	28*	24*
4.75	44*	40	40	36*	32*	32*	28*	28*
5.00	44*	42	42	36*	36*	32*	32*	32*

45 " WIDE FABRIC

TEMPLATE CODES

YARDS	R265	R266	R267	R268	R269	R270	R271	R272
0.25	2	2	2	2	2	2	2	2
0.50	5*	5*	5*	4	4	4	4	4
0.75	6	6	6	6	6	6	6	6
1.00	10*	10*	10*	8	8	8	8	8
1.25	10	10	10	10	10	10	10	10
1.50	15*	15*	15*	12	12	12	12	12
1.75	20*	15*	15*	15*	15*	15*	14	14
2.00	20*	20*	20*	16	16	16	16	16
2.25	25*	20*	20*	20*	20*	18	18	18
2.50	25*	25*	25*	20	20	20	20	20
2.75	30*	30*	25*	25*	25*	22	22	22
3.00	30*	30*	30*	25*	25*	25*	25*	24
3.25	35*	35*	30*	30*	30*	26	26	26
3.50	40*	35*	35*	30*	30*	30*	28	28
3.75	40*	40*	35*	35*	30*	30*	28	28
4.00	45*	40*	40*	35*	35*	35*	32	32
4.25	45*	45*	40*	40*	36	36	36	36
4.50	50*	45*	45*	40*	40*	38	38	38
4.75	55*	50*	45*	45*	40	40	40	40
5.00	55*	50*	50*	45*	45*	42	42	42

36 " WIDE FABRIC

TEMPLATE CODES

YARDS	R273	R274	R275	R276	R277	R278	R279	R280
0.25	1	1	1	3	3	2	2	2
0.50	2	2	2	6	6	4	4	4
0.75	4*	4*	4*	9	9	8*	6	6
1.00	4	4	4	12	12	8	8	8
1.25	5	5	5	16*	15	12*	12*	12*
1.50	8*	8*	8*	18	18	16*	12	12
1.75	8*	8*	8*	21	21	16*	16*	16*
2.00	12*	8	8	24	24	20*	20*	16
2.25	12*	12*	12*	28*	27	24*	20*	20*
2.50	12*	12*	12*	32*	30	24*	24*	24*
2.75	16*	16*	12*	36*	33	28*	28*	24*
3.00	16*	16*	16*	36	36	32*	28*	28*
3.25	16*	16*	16*	40*	39	36*	32*	28*
3.50	20*	20*	16*	44*	42	36*	36*	32*
3.75	20*	20*	20*	48*	45	40*	36*	36*
4.00	24*	20*	20*	52*	48	44*	40*	36*
4.25	24*	24*	24*	52*	51	44*	40*	40*
4.50	24*	24*	24*	56*	54	48*	44*	40*
4.75	28*	24*	24*	60*	57	52*	48*	44*
5.00	28*	28*	28*	64*	60	52*	48*	48*

45 " WIDE FABRIC

TEMPLATE CODES

YARDS	R273	R274	R275	R276	R277	R278	R279	R280
0.25	1	1	1	4	3	3	3	3
0.50	2	2	2	8	6	6	6	6
0.75	5*	5*	5*	12	10*	10*	9	9
1.00	5*	5*	5*	16	15*	12	12	12
1.25	5	5	5	20	15	15	15	15
1.50	10*	10*	10*	24	20*	20*	18	18
1.75	10*	10*	10*	28	25*	21	21	21
2.00	15*	10*	10*	32	30*	25*	25*	24
2.25	15*	15*	15*	36	30*	30*	27	27
2.50	15*	15*	15*	40	35*	30	30	30
2.75	20*	20*	15*	45*	40*	35*	35*	33
3.00	20*	20*	20*	48	45*	40*	36	36
3.25	20*	20*	20*	52	45*	45*	40*	39
3.50	25*	25*	20*	56	50*	45*	45*	42
3.75	25*	25*	25*	60	55*	50*	45	45
4.00	30*	25*	25*	65*	60*	55*	50*	48
4.25	30*	30*	30*	68	60*	55*	51	51
4.50	30*	30*	30*	72	65*	60*	55*	54
4.75	35*	30*	30*	76	70*	65*	60*	57
5.00	35*	35*	35*	80	75*	65*	60	60

36 " WIDE FABRIC

TEMPLATE CODES

YARDS	R281	R282	R283	R284	R285	R286	R287	R288
0.25	2	2	2	1	1	1	1	1
0.50	4	4	4	2	2	2	2	2
0.75	6	6	6	4*	4*	4*	4*	4*
1.00	8	8	8	4	4	4	4	4
1.25	10	10	10	8*	8*	8*	8*	5
1.50	12	12	12	8*	8*	8*	8*	8*
1.75	14	14	14	12*	12*	12*	8*	8*
2.00	16	16	16	12*	12*	12*	12*	12*
2.25	20*	18	18	16*	16*	12*	12*	12*
2.50	20	20	20	16*	16*	16*	16*	12*
2.75	24*	22	22	20*	16*	16*	16*	16*
3.00	24	24	24	20*	20*	20*	16*	16*
3.25	28*	26	26	24*	20*	20*	20*	20*
3.50	28	28	28	24*	24*	24*	20*	20*
3.75	32*	30	30	28*	24*	24*	24*	20*
4.00	36*	32	32	28*	28*	24*	24*	24*
4.25	36*	36*	34	32*	28*	28*	24*	24*
4.50	40*	36	36	32*	32*	28*	28*	28*
4.75	40*	40*	38	36*	32*	32*	28*	28*
5.00	44*	40	40	36*	36*	32*	32*	28*

45 " WIDE FABRIC

TEMPLATE CODES

YARDS	R281	R282	R283	R284	R285	R286	R287	R288
0.25	2	2	2	2	2	2	2	1
0.50	5*	5*	5*	4	4	4	4	2
0.75	6	6	6	6	6	6	6	5*
1.00	10*	10*	10*	8	8	8	8	5*
1.25	10	10	10	10	10	10	10	5
1.50	15*	15*	15*	12	12	12	12	10*
1.75	15*	15*	15*	15*	15*	15*	14	10*
2.00	20*	20*	20*	16	16	16	16	15*
2.25	25*	20*	20*	20*	20*	18	18	15*
2.50	25*	25*	25*	20	20	20	20	15*
2.75	30*	25*	25*	25*	22	22	22	20*
3.00	30*	30*	30*	25*	25*	25*	24	20*
3.25	35*	30*	30*	30*	26	26	26	25*
3.50	35*	35*	35*	30*	30*	30*	28	25*
3.75	40*	35*	35*	35*	30	30	30	25*
4.00	45*	40*	40*	35*	35*	32	32	30*
4.25	45*	45*	40*	40*	35*	35*	34	30*
4.50	50*	45*	45*	40*	40*	36	36	35*
4.75	50*	50*	45*	45*	40*	40*	38	35*
5.00	55*	50*	50*	45*	45*	40	40	35*

36 " WIDE FABRIC

TEMPLATE CODES

YARDS	R289	R290	R291	R292	R293	R294	R295	R296
0.25	1	1	1	0	0	0	0	0
0.50	2	2	2	3	3*	3*	3*	3*
0.75	4*	4*	4*	6	6*	6*	4	4
1.00	4	4	4	9	6	6	6	6
1.25	5	5	5	12	9*	9*	9*	8
1.50	8*	8*	8*	15	12*	12*	10	10
1.75	8*	8*	8*	18	15*	12	12	12
2.00	12*	8	8	21	15*	15*	14	14
2.25	12*	12*	12*	24	18*	18*	16	16
2.50	12*	12*	12*	27	21*	18	18	18
2.75	16*	12*	12*	30	21*	21*	20	20
3.00	16*	16*	16*	33	24*	24*	22	22
3.25	16*	16*	16*	36	27*	24	24	24
3.50	20*	20*	16*	39	30*	27*	26	26
3.75	20*	20*	20*	42	30*	30*	28	28
4.00	24*	20*	20*	45	33*	30	30	30
4.25	24*	24*	20*	48	36*	33*	32	32
4.50	24*	24*	24*	51	36*	36*	34	34
4.75	28*	24*	24*	54	39*	36	36	36
5.00	28*	28*	24*	54	42*	39*	36	36

45 " WIDE FABRIC

TEMPLATE CODES

YARDS	R289	R290	R291	R292	R293	R294	R295	R296
0.25	1	1	1	0	0	0	0	0
0.50	2	2	2	4*	4*	4*	4*	4*
0.75	5*	5*	5*	8*	8*	8*	6	4
1.00	5*	5*	5*	12*	9	9	9	8*
1.25	5	5	5	12	12	12	12	8
1.50	10*	10*	10*	16*	16*	16*	15	12*
1.75	10*	10*	10*	20*	20*	18	18	16*
2.00	15*	10*	10*	24*	21	21	21	16*
2.25	15*	15*	15*	28*	24	24	24	20*
2.50	15*	15*	15*	28*	28*	27	27	20*
2.75	20*	15*	15*	32*	30	30	30	24*
3.00	20*	20*	20*	36*	33	33	33	24*
3.25	20*	20*	20*	40*	36	36	36	28*
3.50	25*	25*	20*	40*	40*	39	39	32*
3.75	25*	25*	25*	44*	42	42	42	32*
4.00	30*	25*	25*	48*	45	45	45	36*
4.25	30*	30*	25*	52*	48	48	48	36*
4.50	30*	30*	30*	56*	51	51	51	40*
4.75	35*	30*	30*	56*	54	54	54	44*
5.00	35*	35*	30*	60*	56*	54	54	44*

36 " WIDE FABRIC

TEMPLATE CODES

YARDS	R297	R298	R299	R300	R301	R302	R303	R304
0.25	0	0	0	0	0	0	0	0
0.50	3*	3*	1	1	1	1	1	1
0.75	4	4	3*	3*	3*	3*	3*	3*
1.00	6	6	3	3	3	3	3	3
1.25	8	8	6*	6*	6*	6*	6*	4
1.50	10	10	6*	6*	6*	6*	6*	6*
1.75	12	12	9*	9*	9*	6	6	6
2.00	14	14	9*	9*	9*	9*	9*	9*
2.25	16	16	12*	12*	9*	9*	9*	9*
2.50	18	18	12*	12*	12*	12*	12*	9
2.75	20	20	15*	15*	12*	12*	12*	12*
3.00	22	22	15*	15*	15*	15*	12*	12*
3.25	24	24	18*	18*	15*	15*	15*	12
3.50	26	26	18*	18*	18*	15*	15*	15*
3.75	28	28	21*	18*	18*	18*	18*	15*
4.00	30	30	21*	21*	21*	18*	18*	18*
4.25	32	32	24*	21*	21*	21*	18*	18*
4.50	34	34	24*	24*	21*	21*	21*	18*
4.75	36	36	27*	24*	24*	21*	21*	21*
5.00	36	36	27*	27*	24*	24*	24*	21*

45 " WIDE FABRIC

TEMPLATE CODES

YARDS	R297	R298	R299	R300	R301	R302	R303	R304
0.25	0	0	0	0	0	0	0	0
0.50	4*	4*	2	2	2	2	2	1
0.75	4	4	4	4	4	4	4	4*
1.00	8*	8*	6	6	6	6	6	4*
1.25	8	8	8	8	8	8	8	4
1.50	12*	12*	10	10	10	10	10	8*
1.75	12	12	12	12	12	12	12	8*
2.00	16*	16*	14	14	14	14	14	12*
2.25	16	16	16	16	16	16	16	12*
2.50	20*	20*	18	18	18	18	18	12*
2.75	24*	20	20	20	20	20	20	16*
3.00	24*	24*	22	22	22	22	22	16*
3.25	28*	24	24	24	24	24	24	16*
3.50	28*	28*	26	26	26	26	26	20*
3.75	32*	28	28	28	28	28	28	20*
4.00	32*	32*	30	30	30	30	30	24*
4.25	36*	32	32	32	32	32	32	24*
4.50	36*	36*	34	34	34	34	34	24*
4.75	40*	36	36	36	36	36	36	28*
5.00	40*	40*	36	36	36	36	36	28*

36 " WIDE FABRIC

TEMPLATE CODES

YARDS	R305	R306	R307	R308	R309	R310	R311	R312
0.25	0	0	0	0	0	0	0	0
0.50	1	1	3*	3*	3*	3*	3*	3*
0.75	3*	3*	6*	4	4	4	4	4
1.00	3	3	6	6	6	6	6	6
1.25	4	4	9*	9*	9*	8	8	8
1.50	6*	6*	12*	10	10	10	10	10
1.75	6	6	12	12	12	12	12	12
2.00	7	7	15*	15*	14	14	14	14
2.25	9*	9*	18*	16	16	16	16	16
2.50	9	9	18	18	18	18	18	18
2.75	12*	10	21*	21*	18	18	18	18
3.00	12*	12*	24*	21*	21*	20	20	20
3.25	12	12	27*	24*	22	22	22	22
3.50	15*	13	27*	27*	24	24	24	24
3.75	15*	15*	30*	27*	27*	26	26	26
4.00	15	15	33*	30*	28	28	28	28
4.25	18*	18*	33*	30	30	30	30	30
4.50	18*	18*	36*	33*	32	32	32	32
4.75	18	18	39*	36*	34	34	34	34
5.00	21*	21*	39*	36	36	36	36	36

45 " WIDE FABRIC

TEMPLATE CODES

YARDS	R305	R306	R307	R308	R309	R310	R311	R312
0.25	0	0	0	0	0	0	0	0
0.50	1	1	4*	4*	4*	4*	4*	4*
0.75	4*	4*	8*	6	6	4	4	4
1.00	4*	4*	9	9	9	8*	8*	8*
1.25	4	4	12	12	12	8	8	8
1.50	8*	8*	16*	15	15	12*	12*	12*
1.75	8*	8*	18	18	18	12	12	12
2.00	8*	8*	21	21	21	16*	16*	16*
2.25	12*	12*	24	24	24	20*	16	16
2.50	12*	12*	27	27	27	20*	20*	20*
2.75	16*	12*	28*	28*	27	24*	20*	20*
3.00	16*	16*	32*	30	30	24*	24*	24*
3.25	16*	16*	36*	33	33	28*	24*	24*
3.50	20*	16*	36	36	36	28*	28*	28*
3.75	20*	20*	40*	39	39	32*	28*	28*
4.00	20*	20*	44*	42	42	36*	32*	32*
4.25	24*	24*	45	45	45	36*	36*	32*
4.50	24*	24*	48	48	48	40*	36*	36*
4.75	24*	24*	52*	51	51	40*	40*	36*
5.00	28*	28*	54	54	54	44*	40*	40*

36 " WIDE FABRIC

TEMPLATE CODES

YARDS	R313	R314	R315	R316	R317	R318	R319	R320
0.25	0	0	0	0	0	0	0	0
0.50	1	1	1	1	1	1	1	1
0.75	3*	3*	3*	3*	3*	3*	3*	3*
1.00	3	3	3	3	3	3	3	3
1.25	6*	6*	6*	6*	4	4	4	4
1.50	6*	6*	6*	6*	6*	6*	6*	6*
1.75	9*	9*	9*	6	6	6	6	6
2.00	9*	9*	9*	9*	9*	9*	7	7
2.25	12*	12*	9*	9*	9*	9*	9*	9*
2.50	12*	12*	12*	12*	9	9	9	9
2.75	15*	12*	12*	12*	12*	12*	9	9
3.00	15*	15*	15*	12*	12*	12*	12*	12*
3.25	18*	15*	15*	15*	15*	12*	12*	12*
3.50	18*	18*	18*	15*	15*	15*	15*	12
3.75	21*	18*	18*	18*	15*	15*	15*	15*
4.00	21*	21*	18*	18*	18*	18*	15*	15*
4.25	24*	21*	21*	18*	18*	18*	18*	15
4.50	24*	24*	21*	21*	21*	18*	18*	18*
4.75	27*	24*	24*	21*	21*	21*	18*	18*
5.00	27*	27*	24*	24*	21*	21*	21*	18

45 " WIDE FABRIC

TEMPLATE CODES

YARDS	R313	R314	R315	R316	R317	R318	R319	R320
0.25	0	0	0	0	0	0	0	0
0.50	2	2	2	2	1	1	1	1
0.75	4	4	4	4	4*	4*	4*	4*
1.00	6	6	6	6	4*	4*	4*	4*
1.25	8	8	8	8	4	4	4	4
1.50	10	10	10	10	8*	8*	8*	8*
1.75	12	12	12	12	8*	8*	8*	8*
2.00	14	14	14	14	12*	12*	8*	8*
2.25	16	16	16	16	12*	12*	12*	12*
2.50	18	18	18	18	12*	12*	12*	12*
2.75	20*	18	18	18	16*	16*	12*	12*
3.00	20	20	20	20	16*	16*	16*	16*
3.25	24*	22	22	22	20*	16*	16*	16*
3.50	24	24	24	24	20*	20*	20*	16*
3.75	28*	26	26	26	20*	20*	20*	20*
4.00	28	28	28	28	24*	24*	20*	20*
4.25	32*	30	30	30	24*	24*	24*	20*
4.50	32	32	32	32	28*	24*	24*	24*
4.75	36*	34	34	34	28*	28*	24*	24*
5.00	36	36	36	36	28*	28*	28*	24*

36 " WIDE FABRIC

TEMPLATE CODES

YARDS	R321	R322	R323	R324	R325	R326	R327	R328
0.25	0	0	0	0	0	0	0	0
0.50	3*	3*	3*	3*	3*	1	1	1
0.75	6*	4	4	4	4	3*	3*	3*
1.00	6	6	6	6	6	3	3	3
1.25	9*	9*	8	8	8	6*	6*	6*
1.50	12*	10	10	10	10	6*	6*	6*
1.75	12	12	12	12	12	9*	9*	9*
2.00	15*	12	12	12	12	9*	9*	9*
2.25	18*	15*	15*	14	14	12*	12*	9*
2.50	18*	18*	16	16	16	12*	12*	12*
2.75	21*	18	18	18	18	15*	15*	12*
3.00	24*	21*	20	20	20	15*	15*	15*
3.25	24*	24*	22	22	22	18*	18*	15*
3.50	27*	24	24	24	24	18*	18*	18*
3.75	30*	27*	24	24	24	21*	18*	18*
4.00	30*	27*	27*	26	26	21*	21*	21*
4.25	33*	30*	28	28	28	24*	21*	21*
4.50	36*	33*	30	30	30	24*	24*	21*
4.75	36*	33*	33*	32	32	27*	24*	24*
5.00	39*	36*	34	34	34	27*	27*	24*

45 " WIDE FABRIC

TEMPLATE CODES

YARDS	R321	R322	R323	R324	R325	R326	R327	R328
0.25	0	0	0	0	0	0	0	0
0.50	4*	4*	4*	4*	4*	2	2	2
0.75	8*	6	4	4	4	4	4	4
1.00	9	9	8*	8*	8*	6	6	6
1.25	12	12	8	8	8	8	8	8
1.50	16*	15	12*	12*	12*	10	12	12
1.75	18	18	16*	12	12	12	12	12
2.00	20*	18	16*	16*	16*	12	12	12
2.25	24*	21	20*	16*	16*	16*	16*	14
2.50	24	24	20*	20*	20*	16	16	16
2.75	28*	27	24*	24*	20*	20*	20*	18
3.00	32*	30	24*	24*	24*	20	20	20
3.25	33	33	28*	28*	28*	24*	24	22
3.50	36	36	32*	28*	28*	24	24	24
3.75	40*	36	32*	32*	28*	28*	24	24
4.00	40*	39	36*	32*	32*	28*	28*	28*
4.25	44*	42	36*	36*	32*	32*	28	28
4.50	48*	45	40*	36*	36*	32*	32*	30
4.75	48	48	44*	40*	36*	36*	32	32
5.00	52*	51	44*	40*	40*	36*	36*	34

36 " WIDE FABRIC

TEMPLATE CODES

YARDS	R329	R330	R331	R332	R333	R334	R335	R336
0.25	0	0	0	0	0	0	0	0
0.50	1	1	1	1	1	3*	3*	3*
0.75	3*	3*	3*	3*	3*	6*	4	4
1.00	3	3	3	3	3	6	6	6
1.25	6*	6*	4	4	4	9*	9*	9*
1.50	6*	6*	6*	6*	6*	12*	9*	9*
1.75	6	6	6	6	6	12*	12*	12*
2.00	9*	9*	9*	6	6	15*	15*	12
2.25	9*	9*	9*	9*	9*	18*	15*	15*
2.50	12*	12*	9*	9*	9*	18*	18*	18*
2.75	12*	12*	12*	12*	9	21*	21*	18
3.00	15*	12*	12*	12*	12*	24*	21*	21*
3.25	15*	15*	12*	12*	12*	27*	24*	21*
3.50	15*	15*	15*	15*	12	27*	27*	24*
3.75	18*	18*	15*	15*	15*	30*	27*	27*
4.00	18*	18*	18*	15*	15*	33*	30*	27*
4.25	21*	18*	18*	18*	18*	33*	30*	30*
4.50	21*	21*	18*	18*	18*	36*	33*	30*
4.75	21*	21*	21*	18*	18*	39*	36*	33*
5.00	24*	24*	21*	21*	21*	39*	36*	36*

45 " WIDE FABRIC

TEMPLATE CODES

YARDS	R329	R330	R331	R332	R333	R334	R335	R336
0.25	0	0	0	0	0	0	0	0
0.50	2	2	1	1	1	4*	4*	4*
0.75	4	4	4*	4*	4*	8*	6	6
1.00	6	6	4*	4*	4*	9	9	9
1.25	8	8	4	4	4	12	12	12
1.50	10	10	8*	8*	8*	16*	12	12
1.75	12	12	8*	8*	8*	16*	16*	16*
2.00	12	12	12*	8*	8*	20*	20*	18
2.25	14	14	12*	12*	12*	24*	21	21
2.50	16	16	12*	12*	12*	24	24	24
2.75	18	18	16*	16*	12*	28*	28*	27
3.00	20	20	16*	16*	16*	32*	28*	28*
3.25	22	22	16*	16*	16*	36*	32*	30
3.50	24	24	20*	20*	16*	36*	36*	33
3.75	24	24	20*	20*	20*	40*	36	36
4.00	26	26	24*	20*	20*	44*	40*	39
4.25	28	28	24*	24*	24*	44*	40*	40*
4.50	30	30	24*	24*	24*	48*	44*	42
4.75	32	32	28*	24*	24*	52*	48*	45
5.00	34	34	28*	28*	28*	52*	48	48

36 " WIDE FABRIC

TEMPLATE CODES

YARDS	R337	R338	R339	R340	R341	R342	R343	R344
0.25	0	0	0	0	0	0	0	0
0.50	3*	3*	3*	1	1	1	1	1
0.75	4	4	4	3*	3*	3*	3*	3*
1.00	6	6	6	3	3	3	3	3
1.25	8	8	8	6*	6*	6*	6*	4
1.50	9*	9*	9*	6*	6*	6*	6*	6*
1.75	10	10	10	9*	9*	9*	6*	6*
2.00	12	12	12	9*	9*	9*	9*	9*
2.25	15*	14	14	12*	12*	9*	9*	9*
2.50	16	16	16	12*	12*	12*	12*	9*
2.75	18	18	18	15*	12*	12*	12*	12*
3.00	18	18	18	15*	15*	15*	12*	12*
3.25	21*	20	20	18*	15*	15*	15*	15*
3.50	22	22	22	18*	18*	18*	15*	15*
3.75	24	24	24	21*	18*	18*	18*	15*
4.00	27*	26	26	21*	21*	18*	18*	18*
4.25	27*	27*	26	24*	21*	21*	18*	18*
4.50	30*	28	28	24*	24*	21*	21*	21*
4.75	30	30	30	27*	24*	24*	21*	21*
5.00	33*	32	32	27*	27*	24*	24*	21*

45 " WIDE FABRIC

TEMPLATE CODES

YARDS	R337	R338	R339	R340	R341	R342	R343	R344
0.25	0	0	0	0	0	0	0	0
0.50	4*	4*	4*	2	2	2	2	1
0.75	4	4	4	4	4	4	4	4*
1.00	8*	8*	8*	6	6	6	6	4*
1.25	8	8	8	8	8	8	8	4
1.50	12*	12*	12*	8	8	8	8	8*
1.75	12*	12*	12*	12*	12*	12*	10	8*
2.00	16*	16*	16*	12	12	12	12	12*
2.25	20*	16*	16*	16*	16*	14	14	12*
2.50	20*	20*	20*	16	16	16	16	12*
2.75	24*	20*	20*	20*	18	18	18	16*
3.00	24*	24*	24*	20*	20*	20*	18	16*
3.25	28*	24*	24*	24*	20	20	20	20*
3.50	28*	28*	28*	24*	24*	24*	22	20*
3.75	32*	28*	28*	28*	24	24	24	20*
4.00	36*	32*	32*	28*	28*	26	26	24*
4.25	36*	36*	32*	32*	28*	28*	26	24*
4.50	40*	36*	36*	32*	32*	28	28	28*
4.75	40*	40*	36*	36*	32*	32*	30	28*
5.00	44*	40*	40*	36*	36*	32	32	28*

```
36 " WIDE FABRIC
```
TEMPLATE CODES

YARDS	R345	R346	R347
0.25	0	0	0
0.50	1	1	1
0.75	3*	3*	3*
1.00	3	3	3
1.25	4	4	4
1.50	6*	6*	6*
1.75	6*	6*	6*
2.00	9*	6	6
2.25	9*	9*	9*
2.50	9*	9*	9*
2.75	12*	9	9
3.00	12*	12*	12*
3.25	12*	12*	12*
3.50	15*	15*	12*
3.75	15*	15*	15*
4.00	18*	15*	15*
4.25	18*	18*	15*
4.50	18*	18*	18*
4.75	21*	18*	18*
5.00	21*	21*	18*

```
45 " WIDE FABRIC
```
TEMPLATE CODES

YARDS	R345	R346	R347
0.25	0	0	0
0.50	1	1	1
0.75	4*	4*	4*
1.00	4*	4*	4*
1.25	4	4	4
1.50	8*	8*	8*
1.75	8*	8*	8*
2.00	12*	8*	8*
2.25	12*	12*	12*
2.50	12*	12*	12*
2.75	16*	12*	12*
3.00	16*	16*	16*
3.25	16*	16*	16*
3.50	20*	20*	16*
3.75	20*	20*	20*
4.00	24*	20*	20*
4.25	24*	24*	20*
4.50	24*	24*	24*
4.75	28*	24*	24*
5.00	28*	28*	24*

Chapter 7

Yardage Charts:
Triangular Templates
(Based on Rectangles)

TRIANGLE TEMPLATE CODES AND MEASUREMENTS
BASED ON RECTANGLES

TEMPLATE CODE	MEASUREMENT WITHOUT SEAM ALLOWANCE (IN INCHES)
T1	1 x 2
T2	1 x 3
T3	1 x 4
T4	1 x 5
T5	1 x 6
T6	1 x 7
T7	1 x 8
T8	1 x 9
T9	1 x 10
T10	1 x 11
T11	1 x 12
T12	1 x 13
T13	1 x 14
T14	1 x 15
T15	1 x 16
T16	1 x 17
T17	1 x 18
T18	1 x 19
T19	1 x 20
T20	1 x 21
T21	1 x 22
T22	1 x 23
T23	1 x 24
T24	1 x 25
T25	1 1/2 x 2 1/2
T26	1 1/2 x 3 1/2
T27	1 1/2 x 4 1/2
T28	1 1/2 x 5 1/2
T29	1 1/2 x 6 1/2
T30	1 1/2 x 7 1/2
T31	1 1/2 x 8 1/2
T32	1 1/2 x 9 1/2
T33	1 1/2 x 10 1/2
T34	1 1/2 x 11 1/2
T35	1 1/2 x 12 1/2
T36	1 1/2 x 13 1/2
T37	1 1/2 x 14 1/2
T38	1 1/2 x 15 1/2
T39	1 1/2 x 16 1/2
T40	1 1/2 x 17 1/2
T41	1 1/2 x 18 1/2

TEMPLATE CODE	MEASUREMENT WITHOUT SEAM ALLOWANCE (IN INCHES)
T42	1 1/2 × 19 1/2
T43	1 1/2 × 20 1/2
T44	1 1/2 × 21 1/2
T45	1 1/2 × 22 1/2
T46	1 1/2 × 23 1/2
T47	1 1/2 × 24 1/2
T48	2 × 4
T49	2 × 5
T50	2 × 6
T51	2 × 7
T52	2 × 8
T53	2 × 9
T54	2 × 10
T55	2 × 11
T56	2 × 12
T57	2 × 13
T58	2 × 14
T59	2 × 15
T60	2 × 16
T61	2 × 17
T62	2 × 18
T63	2 × 19
T64	2 × 20
T65	2 × 21
T66	2 × 22
T67	2 × 23
T68	2 × 24
T69	2 × 25
T70	2 1/2 × 4 1/2
T71	2 1/2 × 5 1/2
T72	2 1/2 × 6 1/2
T73	2 1/2 × 7 1/2
T74	2 1/2 × 8 1/2
T75	2 1/2 × 9 1/2
T76	2 1/2 × 10 1/2
T77	2 1/2 × 11 1/2
T78	2 1/2 × 12 1/2
T79	2 1/2 × 13 1/2
T80	2 1/2 × 14 1/2
T81	2 1/2 × 15 1/2
T82	2 1/2 × 16 1/2

TEMPLATE CODE	MEASUREMENT WITHOUT SEAM ALLOWANCE (IN INCHES)
T83	2 1/2 × 17 1/2
T84	2 1/2 × 18 1/2
T85	2 1/2 × 19 1/2
T86	2 1/2 × 20 1/2
T87	2 1/2 × 21 1/2
T88	2 1/2 × 22 1/2
T89	2 1/2 × 23 1/2
T90	2 1/2 × 24 1/2
T91	3 × 5
T92	3 × 6
T93	3 × 7
T94	3 × 8
T95	3 × 9
T96	3 × 10
T97	3 × 11
T98	3 × 12
T99	3 × 13
T100	3 × 14
T101	3 × 15
T102	3 × 16
T103	3 × 17
T104	3 × 18
T105	3 × 19
T106	3 × 20
T107	3 × 21
T108	3 × 22
T109	3 × 23
T110	3 × 24
T111	3 × 25
T112	3 1/2 × 5 1/2
T113	3 1/2 × 6 1/2
T114	3 1/2 × 7 1/2
T115	3 1/2 × 8 1/2
T116	3 1/2 × 9 1/2
T117	3 1/2 × 10 1/2
T118	3 1/2 × 11 1/2
T119	3 1/2 × 12 1/2
T120	3 1/2 × 13 1/2
T121	3 1/2 × 14 1/2
T122	3 1/2 × 15 1/2
T123	3 1/2 × 16 1/2

TEMPLATE CODE	MEASUREMENT WITHOUT SEAM ALLOWANCE (IN INCHES)
T124	3 1/2 × 17 1/2
T125	3 1/2 × 18 1/2
T126	3 1/2 × 19 1/2
T127	3 1/2 × 20 1/2
T128	3 1/2 × 21 1/2
T129	3 1/2 × 22 1/2
T130	3 1/2 × 23 1/2
T131	3 1/2 × 24 1/2
T132	4 × 6
T133	4 × 7
T134	4 × 8
T135	4 × 9
T136	4 × 10
T137	4 × 11
T138	4 × 12
T139	4 × 13
T140	4 × 14
T141	4 × 15
T142	4 × 16
T143	4 × 17
T144	4 × 18
T145	4 × 19
T146	4 × 20
T147	4 × 21
T148	4 × 22
T149	4 × 23
T150	4 × 24
T151	4 × 25
T152	4 1/2 × 6 1/2
T153	4 1/2 × 7 1/2
T154	4 1/2 × 8 1/2
T155	4 1/2 × 9 1/2
T156	4 1/2 × 10 1/2
T157	4 1/2 × 11 1/2
T158	4 1/2 × 12 1/2
T159	4 1/2 × 13 1/2
T160	4 1/2 × 14 1/2
T161	4 1/2 × 15 1/2
T162	4 1/2 × 16 1/2
T163	4 1/2 × 17 1/2
T164	4 1/2 × 18 1/2

TEMPLATE CODE	MEASUREMENT WITHOUT SEAM ALLOWANCE (IN INCHES)
T165	4 1/2 × 19 1/2
T166	4 1/2 × 20 1/2
T167	4 1/2 × 21 1/2
T168	4 1/2 × 22 1/2
T169	4 1/2 × 23 1/2
T170	4 1/2 × 24 1/2
T171	5 × 7
T172	5 × 8
T173	5 × 9
T174	5 × 10
T175	5 × 11
T176	5 × 12
T177	5 × 13
T178	5 × 14
T179	5 × 15
T180	5 × 16
T181	5 × 17
T182	5 × 18
T183	5 × 19
T184	5 × 20
T185	5 × 21
T186	5 × 22
T187	5 × 23
T188	5 × 24
T189	5 × 25
T190	5 1/2 × 7 1/2
T191	5 1/2 × 8 1/2
T192	5 1/2 × 9 1/2
T193	5 1/2 × 10 1/2
T194	5 1/2 × 11 1/2
T195	5 1/2 × 12 1/2
T196	5 1/2 × 13 1/2
T197	5 1/2 × 14 1/2
T198	5 1/2 × 15 1/2
T199	5 1/2 × 16 1/2
T200	5 1/2 × 17 1/2
T201	5 1/2 × 18 1/2
T202	5 1/2 × 19 1/2
T203	5 1/2 × 20 1/2
T204	5 1/2 × 21 1/2
T205	5 1/2 × 22 1/2

TEMPLATE CODE	MEASUREMENT WITHOUT SEAM ALLOWANCE (IN INCHES)
T206	5 1/2 × 23 1/2
T207	5 1/2 × 24 1/2
T208	6 × 8
T209	6 × 9
T210	6 × 10
T211	6 × 11
T212	6 × 12
T213	6 × 13
T214	6 × 14
T215	6 × 15
T216	6 × 16
T217	6 × 17
T218	6 × 18
T219	6 × 19
T220	6 ×=20
T221	6 × 21
T222	6 × 22
T223	6 × 23
T224	6 × 24
T225	6 × 25
T226	6 1/2 × 8 1/2
T227	6 1/2 × 9 1/2
T228	6 1/2 × 10 1/2
T229	6 1/2 × 11 1/2
T230	6 1/2 × 12 1/2
T231	6 1/2 × 13 1/2
T232	6 1/2 × 14 1/2
T233	6 1/2 × 15 1/2
T234	6 1/2 × 16 1/2
T235	6 1/2 × 17 1/2
T236	6 1/2 × 18 1/2
T237	6 1/2 × 19 1/2
T238	6 1/2 × 20 1/2
T239	6 1/2 × 21 1/2
T240	6 1/2 × 22 1/2
T241	6 1/2 × 23 1/2
T242	6 1/2 × 24 1/2
T243	7 × 9
T244	7 × 10
T245	7 × 11
T246	7 × 12

TEMPLATE CODE	MEASUREMENT WITHOUT SEAM ALLOWANCE (IN INCHES)
T247	7 × 13
T248	7 × 14
T249	7 × 15
T250	7 × 16
T251	7 × 17
T252	7 × 18
T253	7 × 19
T254	7 × 20
T255	7 × 21
T256	7 × 22
T257	7 × 23
T258	7 × 24
T259	7 × 25
T260	7 1/2 × 9 1/2
T261	7 1/2 × 10 1/2
T262	7 1/2 × 11 1/2
T263	7 1/2 × 12 1/2
T264	7 1/2 × 13 1/2
T265	7 1/2 × 14 1/2
T266	7 1/2 × 15 1/2
T267	7 1/2 × 16 1/2
T268	7 1/2 × 17 1/2
T269	7 1/2 × 18 1/2
T270	7 1/2 × 19 1/2
T271	7 1/2 × 20 1/2
T272	7 1/2 × 21 1/2
T273	7 1/2 × 22 1/2
T274	7 1/2 × 23 1/2
T275	7 1/2 × 24 1/2
T276	8 × 10
T277	8 × 11
T278	8 × 12
T279	8 × 13
T280	8 × 14
T281	8 × 15
T282	8 × 16
T283	8 × 17
T284	8 × 18
T285	8 × 19
T286	8 × 20
T287	8 × 21

TEMPLATE CODE	MEASUREMENT WITHOUT SEAM ALLOWANCE (IN INCHES)
T288	8 × 22
T289	8 × 23
T290	8 × 24
T291	8 × 25
T292	8 1/2 × 10 1/2
T293	8 1/2 × 11 1/2
T294	8 1/2 × 12 1/2
T295	8 1/2 × 13 1/2
T296	8 1/2 × 14 1/2
T297	8 1/2 × 15 1/2
T298	8 1/2 × 16 1/2
T299	8 1/2 × 17 1/2
T300	8 1/2 × 18 1/2
T301	8 1/2 × 19 1/2
T302	8 1/2 × 20 1/2
T303	8 1/2 × 21 1/2
T304	8 1/2 × 22 1/2
T305	8 1/2 × 23 1/2
T306	8 1/2 × 24 1/2
T307	9 × 12
T308	9 × 13
T309	9 × 14
T310	9 × 15
T311	9 × 16
T312	9 × 17
T313	9 × 18
T314	9 × 19
T315	9 × 20
T316	9 × 21
T317	9 × 22
T318	9 × 23
T319	9 × 24
T320	9 × 25
T321	9 1/2 × 12 1/2
T322	9 1/2 × 13 1/2
T323	9 1/2 × 14 1/2
T324	9 1/2 × 15 1/2
T325	9 1/2 × 16 1/2
T326	9 1/2 × 17 1/2
T327	9 1/2 × 18 1/2
T328	9 1/2 × 19 1/2

TEMPLATE CODE	MEASUREMENT WITHOUT SEAM ALLOWANCE (IN INCHES)
T329	9 1/2 × 20 1/2
T330	9 1/2 × 21 1/2
T331	9 1/2 × 22 1/2
T332	9 1/2 × 23 1/2
T333	9 1/2 × 24 1/2
T334	10 × 12
T335	10 × 13
T336	10 × 14
T337	10 × 15
T338	10 × 16
T339	10 × 17
T340	10 × 18
T341	10 × 19
T342	10 × 20
T343	10 × 21
T344	10 × 22
T345	10 × 23
T346	10 × 24
T347	10 × 25

36 " WIDE FABRIC

TEMPLATE CODES

YARDS	T1	T2	T3	T4	T5	T6	T7	T8
0.25	42	40	32	24	16	16	16	8
0.50	98	80	64	48	34*	34*	34*	16
0.75	154	128*	96	72	68*	52	52	34*
1.00	210	160	128	102	68	68	68	34
1.25	270*	200	168	136*	102*	102*	84	68*
1.50	330*	256*	200	170*	136*	104	104	68*
1.75	390*	288*	232	174	170*	136*	120	102*
2.00	450*	320	264	204	170*	136	136	102*
2.25	510*	384*	296	238*	204*	170*	156	136*
2.50	570*	416*	336	272*	238*	204*	172	136*
2.75	630*	480*	368	306*	238*	204*	188	170*
3.00	690*	512*	400	340*	272*	238*	208	170*
3.25	750*	544*	432	374*	306*	272*	238*	204*
3.50	810*	608*	464	374*	340*	272*	240	204*
3.75	870*	640*	504	408*	340*	306*	272*	238*
4.00	930*	672*	536	442*	374*	306*	276	238*
4.25	990*	736*	568	476*	408*	340*	306*	272*
4.50	1050*	768*	600	510*	408*	374*	312	272*
4.75	1110*	800*	632	544*	442*	374*	340*	306*
5.00	1140*	864*	672	578*	476*	408*	348	306*

45 " WIDE FABRIC

TEMPLATE CODES

YARDS	T1	T2	T3	T4	T5	T6	T7	T8
0.25	54	48	42*	32	24	24	16	16
0.50	126	96	84*	64	48	48	42*	32
0.75	198	160*	126*	96	84*	78	52	52
1.00	270	200*	168*	136	102	102	84*	68
1.25	342	240	210	168	126	126	84	84
1.50	418*	320*	252*	210*	168*	156	126*	104
1.75	494*	360*	294*	232	210*	180	126*	126*
2.00	570*	400*	336*	272	210*	204	168*	136
2.25	646*	480*	378*	304	252*	234	168*	168*
2.50	722*	520*	420	336	294*	258	210*	172
2.75	798*	600*	462*	378*	294*	282	210*	210*
3.00	874*	640*	504*	420*	336*	312	252*	210*
3.25	950*	680*	546*	462*	378*	336	294*	252*
3.50	1026*	760*	588*	472	420*	360	294*	252*
3.75	1102*	800*	630	504	420*	390	336*	294*
4.00	1178*	840*	672*	546*	462*	414	336*	294*
4.25	1254*	920*	714*	588*	504*	438	378*	336*
4.50	1330*	960*	756*	630*	504*	468	378*	336*
4.75	1406*	1000*	798*	672*	546*	492	420*	378*
5.00	1444*	1080*	882*	714*	588*	516	420*	378*

36 " WIDE FABRIC

TEMPLATE CODES

YARDS	T9	T10	T11	T12	T13	T14	T15	T16
0.25	8	8	8	8	8	8	8	8
0.50	16	16	16	16	16	16	16	16
0.75	34*	34*	34*	34*	26	26	26	26
1.00	34	34	34	34	34	34	34	34
1.25	68*	42	44	44	44	44	44	44
1.50	68*	68*	68*	68*	52	52	52	52
1.75	102*	68*	68*	68*	68*	68*	62	62
2.00	102*	102*	70	70	70	70	70	70
2.25	102*	102*	102*	102*	78	78	78	78
2.50	136*	102*	102*	102*	102*	88	88	88
2.75	136*	136*	136*	102*	102*	102*	102*	96
3.00	170*	136*	136*	136*	106	106	106	106
3.25	170*	170*	136*	136*	136*	114	114	114
3.50	204*	170*	170*	136*	136*	136*	124	124
3.75	204*	170*	170*	170*	136*	136*	136*	132
4.00	238*	204*	170*	170*	170*	140	140	140
4.25	238*	204*	204*	170*	170*	170*	150	150
4.50	238*	238*	204*	204*	170*	170*	158	158
4.75	272*	238*	204*	204*	170*	170*	170*	168
5.00	272*	238*	238*	204*	204*	176	176	176

45 " WIDE FABRIC

TEMPLATE CODES

YARDS	T9	T10	T11	T12	T13	T14	T15	T16
0.25	16	8	8	8	8	8	8	8
0.50	32	16	16	16	16	16	16	16
0.75	52	42*	44*	44*	26	26	26	26
1.00	68	42*	44*	44*	44*	44*	44*	44*
1.25	84	42	44	44	44	44	44	44
1.50	104	84*	88*	88*	52	52	52	52
1.75	126*	84*	88*	88*	88*	88*	62	62
2.00	140	126*	88*	88*	88*	88*	88*	88*
2.25	156	126*	132*	132*	88*	88*	88*	88*
2.50	172	126*	132*	132*	132*	88	88	88
2.75	192	168*	176*	132*	132*	132*	132*	96
3.00	210*	168*	176*	176*	132*	132*	132*	132*
3.25	228	210*	176*	176*	176*	132*	132*	132*
3.50	252*	210*	220*	176*	176*	176*	132*	132*
3.75	260	210*	220*	220*	176*	176*	176*	132
4.00	294*	252*	220*	220*	220*	176*	176*	176*
4.25	296	252*	264*	220*	220*	220*	176*	176*
4.50	312	294*	264*	264*	220*	220*	176*	176*
4.75	336*	294*	264*	264*	220*	220*	176*	176*
5.00	348	294*	308*	264*	264*	220*	220*	220*

36 " WIDE FABRIC

TEMPLATE CODES

YARDS	T17	T18	T19	T20	T21	T22	T23	T24
0.25	0	0	0	0	0	0	0	0
0.50	0	0	0	0	0	0	0	0
0.75	0	0	0	0	0	0	0	0
1.00	0	0	0	0	0	0	0	0
1.25	34*	34*	34*	34*	34*	0	0	0
1.50	34*	34*	34*	34*	34*	34*	34*	34*
1.75	34*	34*	34*	34*	34*	34*	34*	34*
2.00	34*	34*	34*	34*	34*	34*	34*	34*
2.25	68*	68*	34*	34*	34*	34*	34*	34*
2.50	68*	68*	68*	68*	68*	34*	34*	34*
2.75	68*	68*	68*	68*	68*	68*	68*	34*
3.00	68*	68*	68*	68*	68*	68*	68*	68*
3.25	102*	102*	68*	68*	68*	68*	68*	68*
3.50	102*	102*	102*	68*	68*	68*	68*	68*
3.75	102*	102*	102*	102*	102*	68*	68*	68*
4.00	102*	102*	102*	102*	102*	102*	68*	68*
4.25	136*	102*	102*	102*	102*	102*	102*	102*
4.50	136*	136*	102*	102*	102*	102*	102*	102*
4.75	136*	136*	136*	136*	102*	102*	102*	102*
5.00	136*	136*	136*	136*	136*	102*	102*	102*

45 " WIDE FABRIC

TEMPLATE CODES

YARDS	T17	T18	T19	T20	T21	T22	T23	T24
0.25	8	8	8	8	8	0	0	0
0.50	16	16	16	16	16	0	0	0
0.75	26	26	26	26	26	0	0	0
1.00	34	34	34	34	34	0	0	0
1.25	44	44	44	44	44	0	0	0
1.50	52	52	52	52	52	44*	44*	44*
1.75	62	62	62	62	62	44*	44*	44*
2.00	70	70	70	70	70	44*	44*	44*
2.25	88*	88*	78	80	80	44*	44*	44*
2.50	88	88	88	88	88	44*	44*	44*
2.75	96	96	96	96	96	88*	88*	44*
3.00	106	106	106	106	106	88*	88*	88*
3.25	132*	132*	114	114	114	88*	88*	88*
3.50	132*	132*	132*	124	124	88*	88*	88*
3.75	132	132	132	132	132	88*	88*	88*
4.00	140	142	142	142	142	132*	88*	88*
4.25	176*	150	150	150	150	132*	132*	132*
4.50	176*	176*	158	160	160	132*	132*	132*
4.75	176*	176*	176*	176*	168	132*	132*	132*
5.00	176	176	176	176	176	132*	132*	132*

36 " WIDE FABRIC

TEMPLATE CODES

YARDS	T25	T26	T27	T28	T29	T30	T31	T32
0.25	42	30	26*	18	18	12	12	12
0.50	84	60	52*	36	36	26*	26*	26*
0.75	126	104*	80	60	60	52*	40	40
1.00	168	130	104	78	78	52	52	52
1.25	216*	160	130*	104*	102	78*	78*	68
1.50	264*	208*	160	130*	120	104*	80	80
1.75	312*	234*	184	156*	138	104*	104*	96
2.00	336	286*	208	182*	162	130*	108	108
2.25	392	312*	260*	208*	182*	156*	130*	124
2.50	434	338*	286*	234*	204	156*	156*	136
2.75	480*	390*	312*	260*	222	182*	156*	156*
3.00	528*	416*	338*	286*	246	208*	182*	164
3.25	576*	468*	364*	312*	264	208*	182*	182*
3.50	624*	494*	390*	312*	286*	234*	208*	192
3.75	672*	520*	416*	338*	306	260*	234*	208
4.00	696*	572*	442*	364*	324	286*	234*	220
4.25	744*	598*	468*	390*	348	286*	260*	236
4.50	792*	650*	520*	416*	366	312*	286*	248
4.75	840*	676*	546*	442*	390	338*	286*	264
5.00	888*	702*	572*	468*	408	338*	312*	276

45 " WIDE FABRIC

TEMPLATE CODES

YARDS	T25	T26	T27	T28	T29	T30	T31	T32
0.25	54	36	32*	24	18	18	18	12
0.50	108	72	64*	48	36	36	36	34*
0.75	162	128*	100	80	68*	68*	60	40
1.00	216	160*	130	104	102*	78	78	68*
1.25	270	192	160	128	102	102	102	68
1.50	330*	256*	200	160	136*	136*	120	102*
1.75	390*	288*	230	192*	170*	144	144	102*
2.00	432	352*	260	224*	204*	170*	162	136*
2.25	504	384*	320*	256*	238*	204*	186	136*
2.50	558	416*	352*	288*	238*	204	204	170*
2.75	612	480*	384*	320*	272*	238*	228	204*
3.00	666	512*	416*	352*	306*	272*	246	204*
3.25	720	576*	448*	384*	340*	272*	270	238*
3.50	780*	608*	480*	384*	374*	306*	288	238*
3.75	840*	640*	512*	416*	374*	340*	312	272*
4.00	882	704*	544*	448*	408*	374*	330	272*
4.25	954	736*	576*	480*	442*	374*	348	306*
4.50	1008	800*	640*	512*	476*	408*	374*	306*
4.75	1062	832*	672*	544*	510*	442*	390	340*
5.00	1116	864*	704*	576*	510*	442*	414	340*

36 " WIDE FABRIC

TEMPLATE CODES

YARDS	T33	T34	T35	T36	T37	T38	T39	T40
0.25	6	6	6	6	6	6	6	6
0.50	12	14	14	14	14	14	14	14
0.75	26*	28*	28*	28*	28*	28*	20	20
1.00	26	28	28	28	28	28	28	28
1.25	52*	56*	56*	34	34	34	34	34
1.50	52*	56*	56*	56*	56*	56*	42	42
1.75	78*	84*	56*	56*	56*	56*	56*	56*
2.00	78*	84*	84*	84*	56	56	56	56
2.25	104*	112*	84*	84*	84*	84*	62	62
2.50	104*	112*	112*	84*	84*	84*	84*	84*
2.75	130*	140*	112*	112*	112*	84*	84*	84*
3.00	130*	140*	140*	112*	112*	112*	84	84
3.25	156*	140*	140*	140*	112*	112*	112*	90
3.50	156*	168*	140*	140*	140*	112*	112*	112*
3.75	182*	168*	168*	140*	140*	140*	112*	112*
4.00	182*	196*	168*	168*	140*	140*	140*	112
4.25	208*	196*	196*	168*	168*	140*	140*	140*
4.50	208*	224*	196*	196*	168*	168*	140*	140*
4.75	234*	224*	224*	196*	168*	168*	168*	140*
5.00	234*	252*	224*	196*	196*	168*	168*	168*

45 " WIDE FABRIC

TEMPLATE CODES

YARDS	T33	T34	T35	T36	T37	T38	T39	T40
0.25	12	12	12	6	6	6	6	6
0.50	24	28	28	14	14	14	14	14
0.75	40	40	40	34*	34*	34*	20	20
1.00	52	56	56	34*	34*	34*	34*	34*
1.25	68	68	68	34	34	34	34	34
1.50	80	84	84	68*	68*	68*	42	42
1.75	102*	102*	96	68*	68*	68*	68*	68*
2.00	108	112	112	102*	68*	68*	68*	68*
2.25	136*	136*	124	102*	102*	102*	68*	68*
2.50	136	140	140	102*	102*	102*	102*	102*
2.75	170*	170*	152	136*	136*	102*	102*	102*
3.00	170*	170*	170*	136*	136*	136*	102*	102*
3.25	204*	180	180	170*	136*	136*	136*	102*
3.50	204*	204*	196	170*	170*	136*	136*	136*
3.75	238*	208	208	170*	170*	170*	136*	136*
4.00	238*	238*	224	204*	170*	170*	170*	136*
4.25	272*	238*	238*	204*	204*	170*	170*	170*
4.50	272*	272*	252	238*	204*	204*	170*	170*
4.75	306*	272*	272*	238*	204*	204*	204*	170*
5.00	306*	306*	280	238*	238*	204*	204*	204*

36 " WIDE FABRIC

TEMPLATE CODES

YARDS	T49	T50	T51	T52	T53	T54	T55	T56
0.25	22*	12	12	8	8	8	8	4
0.50	44*	30	30'	22*	22*	22*	22*	10
0.75	66*	48	48	44*	32	32	32	22*
1.00	88	66	66	44	44	44	44	22
1.25	110*	88*	88*	66*	66*	56	56	44*
1.50	132*	110*	102	88*	68	68	68	44*
1.75	154*	132*	114	110*	88*	88*	80	66*
2.00	176	154*	132	110*	110*	92	92	66*
2.25	220*	176*	154*	132*	110*	110*	104	88*
2.50	242*	198*	176*	154*	132*	112	116	88*
2.75	264*	220*	186	154*	154*	132*	124	110*
3.00	286*	242*	204	176*	154*	136	136	110*
3.25	308*	264*	220*	198*	176*	154*	148	132*
3.50	330*	286*	242*	220*	176*	176*	160	132*
3.75	352*	308*	264*	220*	198*	176*	172	154*
4.00	374*	330*	286*	242*	220*	198*	184	154*
4.25	396*	330*	288	264*	220*	198*	196	176*
4.50	440*	352*	308*	264*	242*	220*	208	176*
4.75	462*	374*	330*	286*	264*	220*	220	198*
5.00	484*	396*	352*	308*	264*	242*	232	198*

45 " WIDE FABRIC

TEMPLATE CODES

YARDS	T49	T50	T51	T52	T53	T54	T55	T56
0.25	26*	16	16	12	12	8	8	8
0.50	52*	40	40	30	30	28*	28*	20
0.75	80	64	64	56*	48	32	32	32
1.00	110	88	88	66	66	56*	56*	44
1.25	130	112	112	84	84	56	56	56
1.50	160	140*	136	112*	102	84*	84*	68
1.75	190	168*	152	140*	120	112*	84*	84*
2.00	220	196*	176	140*	140*	112*	112*	92
2.25	260*	224*	200	168*	150	140*	112*	112*
2.50	286*	252*	224	196*	168	140*	140*	116
2.75	312*	280*	248	196*	196*	168*	140*	140*
3.00	338*	308*	272	224*	204	168*	168*	140*
3.25	364*	336*	288	252*	224*	196*	168*	168*
3.50	390*	364*	312	280*	240	224*	196*	168*
3.75	416*	392*	336	280*	258	224*	196*	196*
4.00	442*	420*	364*	308*	280*	252*	224*	196*
4.25	470	420*	384	336*	288	252*	224*	224*
4.50	520*	448*	408	336*	308*	280*	252*	224*
4.75	546*	476*	432	364*	336*	280*	280*	252*
5.00	572*	504*	448	392*	342	308*	280*	252*

36 " WIDE FABRIC

TEMPLATE CODES

YARDS	T57	T58	T59	T60	T61	T62	T63	T64
0.25	4	4	4	4	4	4	4	4
0.50	10	10	10	10	10	10	10	10
0.75	22✳	22✳	22✳	22✳	22✳	16	16	16
1.00	22	22	22	22	22	22	22	22
1.25	44✳	44✳	28	28	28	28	28	28
1.50	44✳	44✳	44✳	44✳	44✳	34	34	34
1.75	66✳	44✳	44✳	44✳	44✳	44✳	44✳	44✳
2.00	66✳	66✳	66✳	46	46	46	46	46
2.25	88✳	66✳	66✳	66✳	66✳	52	52	52
2.50	88✳	88✳	66✳	66✳	66✳	66✳	66✳	58
2.75	88✳	88✳	88✳	88✳	66✳	66✳	66✳	66✳
3.00	110✳	110✳	88✳	88✳	88✳	70	70	70
3.25	110✳	110✳	110✳	88✳	88✳	88✳	88✳	76
3.50	132✳	110✳	110✳	110✳	88✳	88✳	88✳	88✳
3.75	132✳	132✳	110✳	110✳	110✳	88	88	88
4.00	154✳	132✳	132✳	110✳	110✳	110✳	94	94
4.25	154✳	154✳	132✳	132✳	110✳	110✳	110✳	110✳
4.50	176✳	154✳	154✳	132✳	132✳	110✳	110✳	110✳
4.75	176✳	154✳	154✳	132✳	132✳	132✳	110	112
5.00	176✳	176✳	154✳	154✳	132✳	132✳	132✳	116

45 " WIDE FABRIC

TEMPLATE CODES

YARDS	T57	T58	T59	T60	T61	T62	T63	T64
0.25	8	8	4	4	4	4	4	4
0.50	20	20	10	10	10	10	10	10
0.75	32	32	28✳	28✳	28✳	16	16	16
1.00	44	44	28✳	28✳	28✳	28✳	28✳	28✳
1.25	56	56	28	28	28	28	28	28
1.50	68	68	56✳	56✳	56✳	34	34	34
1.75	84✳	80	56✳	56✳	56✳	56✳	56✳	56✳
2.00	92	92	84✳	56✳	56✳	56✳	56✳	56✳
2.25	112✳	104	84✳	84✳	84✳	56✳	56✳	56✳
2.50	116	116	84✳	84✳	84✳	84✳	84✳	58
2.75	128	128	112✳	112✳	84✳	84✳	84✳	84✳
3.00	140	140	112✳	112✳	112✳	84✳	84✳	84✳
3.25	148	152	140✳	112✳	112✳	112✳	112✳	84✳
3.50	168✳	160	140✳	140✳	112✳	112✳	112✳	112✳
3.75	172	172	140✳	140✳	140✳	112✳	112✳	112✳
4.00	196✳	184	168✳	140✳	140✳	140✳	112✳	112✳
4.25	196	196	168✳	168✳	140✳	140✳	140✳	140✳
4.50	224✳	208	196✳	168✳	168✳	140✳	140✳	140✳
4.75	224✳	220	196✳	168✳	168✳	168✳	140✳	140✳
5.00	232	232	196✳	196✳	168✳	168✳	168✳	140✳

36 " WIDE FABRIC

TEMPLATE CODES

YARDS	T65	T66	T67	T68	T69	T70	T71	T72
0.25	4	4	4	0	0	20	18*	12
0.50	10	10	10	0	0	40	36*	24
0.75	16	16	16	0	0	70	56	42
1.00	22	22	22	0	0	90	72	54
1.25	28	28	28	22*	22*	110	90*	72
1.50	34	34	34	22*	22*	140	112	90*
1.75	40	40	40	22*	22*	162*	128	108*
2.00	46	46	46	22*	22*	180	152	126*
2.25	52	52	52	44*	44*	210	168	144*
2.50	58	58	58	44*	44*	230	184	162*
2.75	66*	64	64	44*	44*	252*	208	180*
3.00	70	70	70	44*	44*	280	224	198*
3.25	76	76	76	66*	66*	300	252*	216*
3.50	82	82	82	66*	66*	324*	270*	216*
3.75	88	88	88	66*	66*	350	288*	234*
4.00	94	94	94	66*	66*	370	306*	252*
4.25	100	100	100	88*	88*	396*	324*	270*
4.50	110*	106	106	88*	88*	420	342*	288*
4.75	112	112	112	88*	88*	440	360	306*
5.00	118	118	118	88*	88*	460	378*	324*

45 " WIDE FABRIC

TEMPLATE CODES

YARDS	T65	T66	T67	T68	T69	T70	T71	T72
0.25	4	4	4	4	4	24	22*	16
0.50	10	10	10	10	10	48	44*	32
0.75	16	16	16	16	16	84	70	56
1.00	28*	28*	28*	22	22	110*	90	72
1.25	28	28	28	28	28	132	110	96
1.50	34	34	34	34	34	168	140	120*
1.75	40	40	40	40	40	198*	160	144*
2.00	56*	56*	56*	46	46	220*	190	168*
2.25	56*	56*	56*	56*	56*	252	210	192*
2.50	58	58	58	58	58	276	230	216*
2.75	84*	64	64	64	64	308*	260	240*
3.00	84*	84*	84*	70	70	336	280	264*
3.25	84*	84*	84*	84*	84*	360	308*	288*
3.50	84*	84*	84*	84*	84*	396*	330	288*
3.75	112*	112*	88	88	88	420	352*	312*
4.00	112*	112*	112*	94	94	444	380	336*
4.25	112*	112*	112*	112*	112*	484*	400	360*
4.50	140*	112*	112*	112*	112*	506*	420	384*
4.75	140*	140*	112	112	112	528	450	408*
5.00	140*	140*	140*	118	118	552	470	432*

36 " WIDE FABRIC

TEMPLATE CODES

YARDS	T73	T74	T75	T76	T77	T78	T79	T80
0.25	12	8	8	8	8	4	4	4
0.50	24	18*	18*	18*	18*	8	8	10
0.75	42	36*	28	28	28	18*	18*	20*
1.00	54	36	36	36	36	18	18	20
1.25	72	54*	54*	48	48	36*	36*	40*
1.50	84	72*	56	56	56	36*	36*	40*
1.75	102	90*	72*	72*	68	54*	54*	60*
2.00	114	90*	90*	76	76	54*	54*	60*
2.25	126	108*	90*	90*	88	72*	72*	60*
2.50	144	126*	108*	96	96	72*	72*	80*
2.75	156	126*	126*	108	108	90*	90*	80*
3.00	174	144*	126*	126*	116	90*	90*	100*
3.25	186	162*	144*	128	128	108*	108*	100*
3.50	204	180*	162*	144*	136	108*	108*	120*
3.75	216	180*	162*	148	148	126*	108*	120*
4.00	228	198*	180*	162*	156	126*	126*	120*
4.25	246	216*	198*	180*	168	144*	126*	140*
4.50	258	216*	198*	180*	176	144*	144*	140*
4.75	276	234*	216*	198*	188	162*	144*	160*
5.00	288	252*	216*	198*	196	162*	162*	160*

45 " WIDE FABRIC

TEMPLATE CODES

YARDS	T73	T74	T75	T76	T77	T78	T79	T80
0.25	16	12	12	8	8	8	8	8
0.50	32	24	24	24*	24*	16	16	20
0.75	56	48*	42	28	28	28	28	28
1.00	72	54	54	48*	48*	36	36	40
1.25	96	72	72	48	48	48	48	48
1.50	112	96*	84	72*	72*	56	56	72*
1.75	136	120*	102	96*	72*	72*	72*	72*
2.00	152	120*	120*	96*	96*	76	76	80
2.25	168	144*	132	120*	96*	96*	96*	88
2.50	192	168*	144	120*	120*	96	96	100
2.75	208	168*	168*	144*	120*	120*	120*	108
3.00	232	192*	174	168*	144*	120*	120*	120
3.25	248	216*	192	168*	168*	144*	144*	128
3.50	272	240*	216*	192*	168*	144*	144*	144*
3.75	288	240*	222	192*	192*	168*	148	148
4.00	304	264*	240*	216*	192*	168*	168*	160
4.25	328	288*	264*	240*	216*	192*	168	168
4.50	344	288*	264	240*	216*	192*	192*	180
4.75	368	312*	288*	264*	240*	216*	192*	192*
5.00	384	336*	294	264*	240*	216*	216*	200

36 " WIDE FABRIC

TEMPLATE CODES

YARDS	T81	T82	T83	T84	T85	T86	T87	T88
0.25	4	4	4	4	4	4	4	4
0.50	10	10	10	10	10	10	10	10
0.75	20*	20*	20*	20*	14	14	14	14
1.00	20	20	20	20	20	20	20	20
1.25	40*	24	24	24	24	24	24	24
1.50	40*	40*	40*	40*	30	30	30	30
1.75	40*	40*	40*	40*	40*	40*	40*	34
2.00	60*	60*	40	40	40	40	40	40
2.25	60*	60*	60*	60*	44	44	44	44
2.50	80*	60*	60*	60*	60*	60*	50	50
2.75	80*	80*	60*	60*	60*	60*	60*	60*
3.00	80*	80*	80*	80*	60	60	60	60
3.25	100*	80*	80*	80*	80*	80*	64	64
3.50	100*	100*	100*	80*	80*	80*	80*	70
3.75	120*	100*	100*	100*	80*	80*	80*	80*
4.00	120*	120*	100*	100*	100*	80	80	80*
4.25	120*	120*	120*	100*	100*	100*	84	84
4.50	140*	120*	120*	120*	100*	100*	100*	100*
4.75	140*	140*	120*	120*	120*	100*	100*	100*
5.00	160*	140*	140*	120*	120*	120*	100	100

45 " WIDE FABRIC

TEMPLATE CODES

YARDS	T81	T82	T83	T84	T85	T86	T87	T88
0.25	8	4	4	4	4	4	4	4
0.50	20	10	10	10	10	10	10	10
0.75	28	24*	24*	24*	14	14	14	14
1.00	40	24*	24*	24*	24*	24*	24*	24*
1.25	48	24	24	24	24	24	24	24
1.50	60	48*	48*	48*	30	30	30	30
1.75	68	48*	48*	48*	48*	48*	48*	34
2.00	80	72*	48*	48*	48*	48*	48*	48*
2.25	88	72*	72*	72*	48*	48*	48*	48*
2.50	100	72*	72*	72*	72*	72*	50	50
2.75	108	96*	72*	72*	72*	72*	72*	72*
3.00	120	96*	96*	96*	72*	72*	72*	72*
3.25	128	96*	96*	96*	96*	96*	72*	72*
3.50	140	120*	120*	96*	96*	96*	72*	72*
3.75	148	120*	120*	120*	96*	96*	96*	72*
4.00	160	144*	120*	120*	120*	96*	96*	96*
4.25	168	144*	144*	120*	120*	120*	96*	96*
4.50	180	144*	144*	144*	120*	120*	120*	120*
4.75	188	168*	144*	144*	144*	120*	120*	120*
5.00	200	168*	168*	144*	144*	144*	120*	120*

36 " WIDE FABRIC

TEMPLATE CODES

YARDS	T89	T90	T91	T92	T93	T94	T95	T96
0.25	4	4	16	16	12	12	8	8
0.50	10	10	32	32	24	24	16	16
0.75	14	14	48	48	36	36	32*	24
1.00	20	20	64	64	48	48	32	32
1.25	24	24	96*	80	64*	60	48*	48*
1.50	30	30	112*	96	80*	72	64*	48
1.75	34	34	128*	112	96*	84	80*	64*
2.00	40	40	144*	128	112*	102	80*	80*
2.25	44	44	176*	144	128*	114	96*	80*
2.50	50	50	192*	160	144*	126	112*	96*
2.75	54	54	208*	176	144*	138	112*	112*
3.00	60	60	224*	200	160*	150	128*	112*
3.25	64	64	256*	216	176*	162	144*	128*
3.50	70	70	272*	232	192*	176*	160*	144*
3.75	80*	74	288*	248	208*	186	160*	144*
4.00	80	80	304*	264	224*	204	176*	160*
4.25	86	86	320*	280	240*	216	192*	176*
4.50	90	90	352*	296	256*	228	192*	176*
4.75	100*	96	368*	312	272*	240	208*	192*
5.00	100	100	384*	328	288*	252	224*	192*

45 " WIDE FABRIC

TEMPLATE CODES

YARDS	T89	T90	T91	T92	T93	T94	T95	T96
0.25	4	4	24	20	16	12	12	12
0.50	10	10	48	40	32	24	24	24
0.75	14	14	72	60	48	40*	40*	36
1.00	24*	24*	96	80	64	60*	48	48
1.25	24	24	120	100	80	60	60	60
1.50	30	30	144	120	100*	80*	80*	72
1.75	34	34	168	140	120*	100*	100*	90
2.00	48*	48*	192	160	140*	120*	102	102
2.25	48*	48*	220*	180	160*	140*	120*	114
2.50	50	50	240	200	180*	140*	140*	126
2.75	54	54	264	220	184	160*	140*	140*
3.00	72*	72*	288	250	200	180*	160*	150
3.25	72*	72*	320*	270	220*	200*	180*	168
3.50	72*	72*	340*	290	240*	220*	200*	180
3.75	96*	74	360	310	260*	220*	200*	192
4.00	96*	96*	384	330	280*	240*	220*	204
4.25	96*	96*	408	350	300*	260*	240*	220*
4.50	96*	96*	440*	370	320*	280*	240*	228
4.75	120*	96	468	390	340*	300*	260*	240
5.00	120*	120*	492	410	360*	300*	280*	258

36 " WIDE FABRIC

TEMPLATE CODES

YARDS	T97	T98	T99	T100	T101	T102	T103	T104
0.25	8	8	8	4	4	4	4	4
0.50	16	16	16	8	8	8	8	8
0.75	24	24	24	16*	16*	16*	16*	16*
1.00	32	32	32	16	16	16	16	16
1.25	40	40	40	32*	32*	32*	20	22
1.50	48	52	52	32*	32*	32*	32*	32*
1.75	64*	60	60	48*	48*	32*	32*	32*
2.00	68	68	68	48*	48*	48*	48*	32*
2.25	80*	76	76	64*	48*	48*	48*	34
2.50	84	84	84	64*	64*	48*	48*	48*
2.75	96*	92	92	80*	64*	64*	64*	48*
3.00	112*	104	104	80*	80*	64*	64*	64*
3.25	112	112	112	96*	80*	80*	80*	64*
3.50	128*	120	120	96*	96*	80*	80*	64*
3.75	128	128	128	112*	96*	96*	80*	80*
4.00	144*	136	136	112*	112*	96*	80*	80*
4.25	160*	144	148	112*	112*	96*	96*	80*
4.50	160*	156	156	128*	112*	112*	96*	96*
4.75	176*	164	164	128*	128*	112*	112*	96*
5.00	176*	172	172	144*	128*	128*	112*	112*

45 " WIDE FABRIC

TEMPLATE CODES

YARDS	T97	T98	T99	T100	T101	T102	T103	T104
0.25	8	8	8	8	8	8	4	4
0.50	20*	20*	20*	16	16	16	8	8
0.75	24	24	24	24	24	24	20*	22*
1.00	40*	40*	40*	32	32	32	20*	22*
1.25	40	40	40	40	40	40	20	22
1.50	60*	60*	60*	52	52	52	40*	44*
1.75	80*	60	60	60	60	60	40*	44*
2.00	80*	80*	80*	68	68	68	60*	44*
2.25	100*	80*	80*	80*	76	76	60*	66*
2.50	100*	100*	100*	84	84	84	60*	66*
2.75	120*	100*	100*	100*	96	96	80*	88*
3.00	140*	120*	120*	104	104	104	80*	88*
3.25	140*	140*	120*	120*	112	112	100*	88*
3.50	160*	140*	140*	120	120	120	100*	88*
3.75	160*	160*	140*	140*	128	128	100*	110*
4.00	180*	160*	160*	140*	140	140	120*	110*
4.25	200*	180*	160*	148	148	148	120*	132*
4.50	200*	180*	180*	160*	156	156	120*	132*
4.75	220*	200*	180*	164	164	164	140*	132*
5.00	220*	200*	200*	180*	172	172	140*	154*

36 " WIDE FABRIC

TEMPLATE CODES

YARDS	T105	T106	T107	T108	T109	T110	T111	T112
0.25	4	4	4	4	4	4	4	14*
0.50	8	8	8	8	8	8	8	28*
0.75	16*	12	12	12	12	12	12	42*
1.00	16	16	16	16	16	16	16	56
1.25	22	22	22	22	22	22	22	72
1.50	32*	26	26	26	26	26	26	84*
1.75	32*	32*	32*	32*	32*	30	30	112*
2.00	34	34	34	34	34	34	34	126*
2.25	48*	38	38	38	38	38	38	140*
2.50	48*	48*	48*	48*	44	44	44	154*
2.75	48	48	48	48	48	48	48	168*
3.00	64*	52	52	52	52	52	52	182*
3.25	64*	64*	64*	56	56	56	56	210*
3.50	64*	64*	64*	64*	64*	60	62	224*
3.75	80*	66	66	66	66	66	66	238*
4.00	80*	80*	80*	70	70	70	70	252*
4.25	80*	80*	80*	80*	74	74	74	266*
4.50	96*	80*	80*	80*	80*	78	78	280*
4.75	96*	96*	82	82	84	84	84	308*
5.00	96*	96*	96*	96*	88	88	88	322*

45 " WIDE FABRIC

TEMPLATE CODES

YARDS	T105	T106	T107	T108	T109	T110	T111	T112
0.25	4	4	4	4	4	4	4	18*
0.50	8	8	8	8	8	8	8	36*
0.75	22*	12	12	12	12	12	12	54*
1.00	22*	22*	22*	22*	22*	22*	22*	72*
1.25	22	22	22	22	22	22	22	90
1.50	44*	26	26	26	26	26	26	108*
1.75	44*	44*	44*	44*	44*	30	30	144*
2.00	44*	44*	44*	44*	44*	44*	44*	162*
2.25	66*	44*	44*	44*	44*	44*	44*	180*
2.50	66*	66*	66*	66*	44	44	44	198*
2.75	66*	66*	66*	66*	66*	66*	48	216*
3.00	88*	66*	66*	66*	66*	66*	66*	234*
3.25	88*	88*	88*	66*	66*	66*	66*	270*
3.50	88*	88*	88*	88*	88*	66*	66*	288*
3.75	110*	88*	88*	88*	88*	88*	66	306*
4.00	110*	110*	110*	88*	88*	88*	88*	324*
4.25	110*	110*	110*	110*	88*	88*	88*	342*
4.50	132*	110*	110*	110*	110*	88*	88*	360*
4.75	132*	132*	110*	110*	110*	110*	110*	396*
5.00	132*	132*	132*	132*	110*	110*	110*	414*

36 " WIDE FABRIC

TEMPLATE CODES

YARDS	T113	T114	T115	T116	T117	T118	T119	T120
0.25	14*	6	6	4	4	4	4	4
0.50	28*	18	18	14*	14*	14*	14*	14*
0.75	42*	30	30	28*	20	20	20	20
1.00	56	42	42	28	28	28	28	28
1.25	72	56*	54	42*	42*	36	36	36
1.50	88	70*	66	56*	44	44	44	44
1.75	104	84*	78	56*	56*	56*	52	52
2.00	112	98*	90	70*	70*	60	60	60
2.25	128	98*	102	84*	70*	70*	68	68
2.50	144	112*	108	98*	84*	76	76	76
2.75	160	126*	120	98*	98*	84	84	84
3.00	176	140*	132	112*	98*	98*	92	92
3.25	192	154*	144	126*	112*	100	100	100
3.50	208	168*	156	126*	112*	112*	108	108
3.75	216	182*	168	140*	126*	112	112	116
4.00	232	196*	180	154*	140*	126*	120	120
4.25	248	196*	192	154*	140*	128	128	128
4.50	264	210*	204	168*	154*	140*	136	136
4.75	280	224*	216	182*	168*	154*	144	144
5.00	296	238*	222	196*	168*	154*	152	152

45 " WIDE FABRIC

TEMPLATE CODES

YARDS	T113	T114	T115	T116	T117	T118	T119	T120
0.25	18*	8	6	6	6	4	4	4
0.50	36*	24	18	18	18	18*	18*	18*
0.75	54*	40	36*	36*	30	20	20	20
1.00	72*	56	54*	42	42	36*	36*	36*
1.25	90	72	54	54	54	36	36	36
1.50	110	90*	72*	72*	66	54*	54*	54*
1.75	130	108*	90*	78	78	72*	54*	54*
2.00	144*	126*	108*	90	90	72*	72*	72*
2.25	162*	128	126*	108*	102	90*	72*	72*
2.50	180	144	126*	126*	114	90*	90*	90*
2.75	200	162*	144*	126*	126	108*	90*	90*
3.00	220	180*	162*	144*	138	126*	108*	108*
3.25	240	198*	180*	162*	144	126*	126*	108*
3.50	260	216*	180*	162*	156	144*	126*	126*
3.75	270	234*	198*	180*	168	144*	144*	126*
4.00	290	252*	216*	198*	180	162*	144*	144*
4.25	310	252*	234*	198*	192	162*	162*	144*
4.50	330	270*	252*	216*	204	180*	162*	162*
4.75	350	288*	252*	234*	216	198*	180*	162*
5.00	370	306*	270*	252*	228	198*	180*	180*

36 " WIDE FABRIC

TEMPLATE CODES

YARDS	T121	T122	T123	T124	T125	T126	T127	T128
0.25	2	2	2	2	2	2	2	2
0.50	6	6	6	6	6	6	6	6
0.75	14*	14*	14*	14*	14*	14*	14*	10
1.00	14	14	14	14	14	14	14	14
1.25	28*	28*	28*	18	18	18	18	18
1.50	28*	28*	28*	28*	28*	28*	28*	22
1.75	42*	42*	28*	28*	28*	28*	28*	28*
2.00	42*	42*	42*	42*	30	30	30	30
2.25	56*	42*	42*	42*	42*	42*	42*	34
2.50	56*	56*	56*	42*	42*	42*	42*	42*
2.75	70*	56*	56*	56*	56*	42	42	42
3.00	70*	70*	56*	56*	56*	56*	56*	46
3.25	84*	70*	70*	70*	56*	56*	56*	56*
3.50	84*	84*	70*	70*	70*	56*	56*	56*
3.75	98*	84*	84*	70*	70*	70*	70*	58
4.00	98*	98*	84*	84*	70*	70*	70*	70*
4.25	98*	98*	98*	84*	84*	70*	70*	70*
4.50	112*	98*	98*	98*	84*	84*	84*	70
4.75	112*	112*	98*	98*	98*	84*	84*	84*
5.00	126*	112*	112*	98*	98*	98*	84*	84*

45 " WIDE FABRIC

TEMPLATE CODES

YARDS	T121	T122	T123	T124	T125	T126	T127	T128
0.25	4	4	4	2	2	2	2	2
0.50	12	12	12	6	6	6	6	6
0.75	20	20	20	18*	18*	18*	18*	10
1.00	28	28	28	18*	18*	18*	18*	18*
1.25	36	36	36	18	18	18	18	18
1.50	44	44	44	36*	36*	36*	36*	22
1.75	54*	54*	52	36*	36*	36*	36*	36*
2.00	60	60	60	54*	36*	36*	36*	36*
2.25	72*	68	68	54*	54*	54*	54*	36*
2.50	76	76	76	54*	54*	54*	54*	54*
2.75	90*	84	84	72*	72*	54*	54*	54*
3.00	92	92	92	72*	72*	72*	72*	54*
3.25	108*	100	100	90*	72*	72*	72*	72*
3.50	108	108	108	90*	90*	72*	72*	72*
3.75	126*	116	116	90*	90*	90*	90*	72*
4.00	126*	126*	124	108*	90*	90*	90*	90*
4.25	132	132	132	108*	108*	90*	90*	90*
4.50	144*	140	140	126*	108*	108*	108*	90*
4.75	144	144	148	126*	126*	108*	108*	108*
5.00	162*	152	152	126*	126*	126*	108*	108*

36 " WIDE FABRIC

TEMPLATE CODES

YARDS	T129	T130	T131	T132	T133	T134	T135	T136
0.25	2	2	2	12*	6	6	6	4
0.50	6	6	6	24	18	18	18	12
0.75	10	10	10	36*	30	30	30	24*
1.00	14	14	14	48	36	36	36	24
1.25	18	18	18	64	48	48	48	36*
1.50	22	22	22	72	60	60	60	48*
1.75	28*	28*	26	88	72*	66	66	48
2.00	30	30	30	104	84*	78	78	60*
2.25	34	34	34	112	96*	90	90	72*
2.50	42*	38	38	132*	108*	96	102	72*
2.75	42	42	42	144	120*	108	108	84*
3.00	46	46	46	156*	132*	120	120	96*
3.25	50	50	50	168	144*	132	132	96*
3.50	56*	56*	54	184	156*	138	138	108*
3.75	58	58	58	192	168*	150	150	120*
4.00	62	62	62	208	180*	162	162	120*
4.25	70*	66	66	224	192*	168	174	132*
4.50	70	70	70	232	204*	180	180	144*
4.75	74	74	74	248	216*	192	192	156*
5.00	84*	78	78	264	228*	198	204	156*

45 " WIDE FABRIC

TEMPLATE CODES

YARDS	T129	T130	T131	T132	T133	T134	T135	T136
0.25	2	2	2	16*	8	8	6	6
0.50	6	6	6	32*	24	24	18	18
0.75	10	10	10	48*	40	40	32*	32*
1.00	18*	18*	18*	64*	48	48	48*	36
1.25	18	18	18	80	64	64	48	48
1.50	22	22	22	96*	80	80	64*	64*
1.75	36*	36*	26	112*	96*	88	80*	72
2.00	36*	36*	36*	130	112*	104	96*	80*
2.25	36*	36*	36*	144*	128*	120	96*	96*
2.50	54*	38	38	176*	144*	128	112*	102
2.75	54*	54*	54*	192*	160*	144	128*	112*
3.00	54*	54*	54*	208*	176*	160	144*	128*
3.25	54*	54*	54*	224*	192*	176	144*	132
3.50	72*	72*	54	240*	208*	184	160*	144
3.75	72*	72*	72*	256*	224*	200	176*	160*
4.00	72*	72*	72*	272*	240*	216	192*	162
4.25	90*	72*	72*	288*	256*	224	192*	176*
4.50	90*	90*	90*	304*	272*	240	208*	192*
4.75	90*	90*	90*	320*	288*	256	224*	208*
5.00	108*	90*	90*	352*	304*	264	240*	208*

36 " WIDE FABRIC

TEMPLATE CODES

YARDS	T137	T138	T139	T140	T141	T142	T143	T144
0.25	4	4	4	2	2	2	2	2
0.50	12	12	12	6	6	6	6	6
0.75	20	20	20	12*	12*	14*	14*	14*
1.00	24	24	24	12	12	14	14	14
1.25	36*	32	32	24*	24*	28*	28*	16
1.50	40	40	40	24*	24*	28*	28*	28*
1.75	48	48	48	36*	36*	42*	28*	28*
2.00	60*	52	52	36*	36*	42*	42*	42*
2.25	60	60	60	48*	48*	42*	42*	42*
2.50	72*	68	68	48*	48*	56*	56*	42*
2.75	72	76	76	60*	60*	56*	56*	56*
3.00	84*	80	80	60*	60*	70*	56*	56*
3.25	96*	88	88	72*	72*	70*	70*	70*
3.50	96	96	96	72*	72*	84*	70*	70*
3.75	108*	100	104	84*	72*	84*	84*	70*
4.00	120*	108	108	84*	84*	98*	84*	84*
4.25	120*	116	116	96*	84*	98*	98*	84*
4.50	132*	124	124	96*	96*	98*	98*	98*
4.75	132*	128	132	108*	96*	112*	98*	98*
5.00	144*	136	136	108*	108*	112*	112*	98*

45 " WIDE FABRIC

TEMPLATE CODES

YARDS	T137	T138	T139	T140	T141	T142	T143	T144
0.25	6	4	4	4	4	4	4	2
0.50	18	16*	16*	12	12	12	12	6
0.75	30	20	20	20	20	20	20	16*
1.00	36	32*	32*	24	24	28	28	16*
1.25	48	32	32	32	32	32	32	16
1.50	60	48*	48*	40	40	40	40	32*
1.75	72	64*	48	48	48	48	48	32*
2.00	80*	64*	64*	52	52	56	56	48*
2.25	90	80*	64*	64*	64*	60	60	48*
2.50	102	80*	80*	68	68	68	68	48*
2.75	108	96*	80*	80*	80*	76	76	64*
3.00	120	96*	96*	80	80	84	84	64*
3.25	132	112*	96*	96*	96*	88	88	80*
3.50	144	128*	112*	96	96	96	96	80*
3.75	150	128*	128*	112*	104	104	104	80*
4.00	162	144*	128*	112*	112*	112	112	96*
4.25	174	144*	144*	128*	116	116	116	96*
4.50	186	160*	144*	128*	128*	124	124	112*
4.75	192	160*	160*	144*	132	132	132	112*
5.00	204	176*	160*	144*	144*	140	140	112*

36 " WIDE FABRIC

TEMPLATE CODES

YARDS	T145	T146	T147	T148	T149	T150	T151	T152
0.25	2	2	2	2	2	2	2	12*
0.50	6	6	6	6	6	6	6	24
0.75	14*	14*	14*	10	10	10	10	36*
1.00	14	14	14	14	14	14	14	48
1.25	16	16	16	16	16	16	16	60*
1.50	28*	28*	28*	20	20	20	20	72
1.75	28*	28*	28*	28*	28*	28*	24	84*
2.00	28	28	28	28	28	28	28	96
2.25	42*	42*	42*	30	30	30	30	108*
2.50	42*	42*	42*	42*	42*	34	34	120
2.75	56*	42*	42*	42*	42*	42*	42*	132*
3.00	56*	56*	56*	42	42	42	42	144
3.25	56*	56*	56*	56*	44	44	46	156*
3.50	70*	56*	56*	56*	56*	56*	48	168
3.75	70*	70*	70*	56*	56*	56*	56*	180*
4.00	70*	70*	70*	70*	56	56	56	192
4.25	84*	70*	70*	70*	70*	70*	60	204*
4.50	84*	84*	84*	70*	70*	70*	70*	216
4.75	98*	84*	84*	84*	70*	70*	70*	228*
5.00	98*	98*	84*	84*	84*	70	70	240

45 " WIDE FABRIC

TEMPLATE CODES

YARDS	T145	T146	T147	T148	T149	T150	T151	T152
0.25	2	2	2	2	2	2	2	14*
0.50	6	6	6	6	6	6	6	30
0.75	16*	16*	16*	10	10	10	10	42*
1.00	16*	16*	16*	16*	16*	16*	16*	60
1.25	16	16	16	16	16	16	16	70
1.50	32*	32*	32*	20	20	20	20	90
1.75	32*	32*	32*	32*	32*	32*	24	100
2.00	32*	32*	32*	32*	32*	32*	32*	120
2.25	48*	48*	48*	32*	32*	32*	32*	130
2.50	48*	48*	48*	48*	48*	34	34	150
2.75	64*	48*	48*	48*	48*	48*	48*	160
3.00	64*	64*	64*	48*	48*	48*	48*	180
3.25	64*	64*	64*	64*	48*	48*	48*	190
3.50	80*	64*	64*	64*	64*	64*	48	210
3.75	80*	80*	80*	64*	64*	64*	64*	220
4.00	80*	80*	80*	80*	64*	64*	64*	240
4.25	96*	80*	80*	80*	80*	80*	64*	250
4.50	96*	96*	96*	80*	80*	80*	80*	270
4.75	112*	96*	96*	96*	80*	80*	80*	280
5.00	112*	112*	96*	96*	96*	80*	80*	300

36 " WIDE FABRIC

TEMPLATE CODES

YARDS	T153	T154	T155	T156	T157	T158	T159	T160
0.25	6	6	4	4	4	4	4	2
0.50	18	18	12	12	12	12	12	6
0.75	24	24	24*	24*	16	16	16	12*
1.00	36	36	24	24	24	24	24	12
1.25	48*	48*	36*	36*	36*	28	28	24*
1.50	60*	54	48*	48*	36	36	36	24*
1.75	72*	60	60*	48*	48*	44	44	36*
2.00	84*	72	60*	60*	48	48	48	36*
2.25	96*	84*	72*	72*	60*	60*	56	48*
2.50	108*	96*	84*	72*	72*	60	60	48*
2.75	120*	96	96*	84*	72*	72*	68	60*
3.00	132*	108	96*	96*	84*	72	72	60*
3.25	132*	120	108*	96*	84*	84*	80	72*
3.50	144*	132*	120*	108*	96*	88	88	72*
3.75	156*	144*	132*	120*	108*	96*	92	84*
4.00	168*	156*	132*	120*	108*	108*	100	84*
4.25	180*	156	144*	132*	120*	108*	104	96*
4.50	192*	168*	156*	144*	132*	120*	112	96*
4.75	204*	180*	156*	144*	132*	120*	120	108*
5.00	216*	192*	168*	156*	144*	132*	124	108*

45 " WIDE FABRIC

TEMPLATE CODES

YARDS	T153	T154	T155	T156	T157	T158	T159	T160
0.25	8	8	6	6	6	4	4	4
0.50	24	24	18	18	18	14*	14*	12
0.75	32	32	28*	28*	24	16	16	16
1.00	48	48	36	36	36	28*	28*	24
1.25	56	56	42	42	42	28	28	28
1.50	72	72	56*	56*	54	42*	42*	36
1.75	84*	80	70*	60	60	44	44	48
2.00	98*	96	72	72	72	56*	56*	48
2.25	112*	104	84*	84	84	70*	56	56
2.50	126*	120	98*	90	90	70*	70*	60
2.75	140*	128	112*	102	102	84*	70*	70*
3.00	154*	144	112*	112*	108	84*	84*	76
3.25	154*	160	126*	120	120	98*	84*	84*
3.50	168	168	140*	126	126	98*	98*	88
3.75	182*	184	154*	140*	138	112*	98*	98*
4.00	196*	192	154*	150	150	126*	112*	100
4.25	210*	208	168*	156	156	126*	112*	112*
4.50	224*	216	182*	168	168	140*	126*	112
4.75	238*	232	182*	174	174	140*	140*	126*
5.00	252*	240	196*	186	186	154*	140*	126*

36 " WIDE FABRIC

TEMPLATE CODES

YARDS	T161	T162	T163	T164	T165	T166	T167	T168
0.25	2	2	2	2	2	2	2	2
0.50	6	6	6	6	6	6	6	6
0.75	12*	12*	12*	12*	12*	12*	12*	8
1.00	12	12	12	12	12	12	12	12
1.25	24*	24*	24*	14	14	16	16	16
1.50	24*	24*	24*	24*	24*	24*	24*	18
1.75	36*	36*	24*	24*	24*	24*	24*	24*
2.00	36*	36*	36*	36*	24	24	24	24
2.25	48*	36*	36*	36*	36*	36*	36*	28
2.50	48*	48*	48*	36*	36*	36*	36*	36*
2.75	60*	48*	48*	48*	48*	36*	36*	36*
3.00	60*	60*	48*	48*	48*	48*	48*	38
3.25	60*	60*	60*	60*	48*	48*	48*	48*
3.50	72*	72*	60*	60*	60*	48*	48*	48*
3.75	72*	72*	72*	60*	60*	60*	60*	48
4.00	84*	72*	72*	72*	60*	60*	60*	60*
4.25	84*	84*	72*	72*	72*	60*	60*	60*
4.50	96*	84*	84*	72*	72*	72*	72*	60*
4.75	96*	96*	84*	84*	84*	72*	72*	72*
5.00	108*	96*	96*	84*	84*	84*	72*	72*

45 " WIDE FABRIC

TEMPLATE CODES

YARDS	T161	T162	T163	T164	T165	T166	T167	T168
0.25	4	4	4	2	2	2	2	2
0.50	12	12	12	6	6	6	6	6
0.75	16	16	16	14*	14*	16*	16*	8
1.00	24	24	24	14*	14*	16*	16*	16*
1.25	28	28	28	14	14	16	16	16
1.50	36	36	36	28*	28*	32*	32*	18
1.75	44	44	44	28*	28*	32*	32*	32*
2.00	48	48	48	42*	28*	32*	32*	32*
2.25	56	56	56	42*	42*	48*	48*	32*
2.50	60	60	60	42*	42*	48*	48*	48*
2.75	70*	68	68	56*	56*	48*	48*	48*
3.00	76	76	76	56*	56*	64*	64*	48*
3.25	80	80	80	70*	56*	64*	64*	64*
3.50	88	88	88	70*	70*	64*	64*	64*
3.75	92	92	92	70*	70*	80*	80*	64*
4.00	100	100	100	84*	70*	80*	80*	80*
4.25	108	108	108	84*	84*	80*	80*	80*
4.50	112	112	112	84*	84*	96*	96*	80*
4.75	120	120	120	98*	98*	96*	96*	96*
5.00	126*	124	124	98*	98*	112*	96*	96*

36 " WIDE FABRIC

TEMPLATE CODES

YARDS	T169	T170	T171	T172	T173	T174	T175	T176
0.25	2	2	6	6	6	4	4	4
0.50	6	6	12	12	12	10*	10*	10*
0.75	8	8	24	24	24	20*	16	16
1.00	12	12	30	30	30	20	20	20
1.25	16	16	40*	42	42	30*	30*	28
1.50	18	18	50*	50*	48	40*	32	32
1.75	24*	24*	60*	60*	54	40*	40	40
2.00	24	24	70*	70*	66	50*	50*	44
2.25	28	28	80*	72	72	60*	50*	50*
2.50	36*	32	90*	84	84	70*	60*	56
2.75	36*	36*	100*	90	90	70*	70*	60
3.00	38	38	110*	100*	102	80*	70*	70*
3.25	40	40	120*	110*	108	90*	80*	72
3.50	48*	48*	130*	120*	114	90*	90*	80
3.75	48	48	140*	130*	126	100*	90*	84
4.00	50	50	150*	140*	132	110*	100*	92
4.25	60*	60*	160*	140*	144	120*	110*	100*
4.50	60*	60*	170*	150	150	120*	110*	100
4.75	60	60	180*	160*	156	130*	120*	110*
5.00	72*	64	190*	170*	168	140*	130*	112

45 " WIDE FABRIC

TEMPLATE CODES

YARDS	T169	T170	T171	T172	T173	T174	T175	T176
0.25	2	2	8	8	6	6	6	4
0.50	6	6	16	16	14*	14*	14*	14*
0.75	8	8	32	32	28*	28*	24	16
1.00	16*	16*	40	42*	42*	30	30	28*
1.25	16	16	48	56	42	42	42	28
1.50	18	18	64	70*	56*	56*	48	42*
1.75	32*	32*	72	84*	70*	56*	60	56*
2.00	32*	32*	88	98*	84*	70*	70*	56*
2.25	32*	32*	96	98*	98*	84*	72	70*
2.50	48*	32	108*	112	98*	98*	84	70*
2.75	48*	48*	120	126*	112*	98*	98*	84*
3.00	48*	48*	132*	140*	126*	112*	102	98*
3.25	48*	48*	144	154*	140*	126*	112*	98*
3.50	64*	64*	156*	168*	154*	126*	126*	112*
3.75	64*	64*	168*	182*	154*	140*	126	112*
4.00	64*	64*	180*	196*	168*	154*	140*	126*
4.25	80*	80*	192*	196*	182*	168*	154*	140*
4.50	80*	80*	204*	210*	196*	168*	154*	140*
4.75	80*	80*	216*	224*	196*	182*	168*	154*
5.00	96*	80*	228*	238*	210*	196*	182*	154*

36 " WIDE FABRIC

TEMPLATE CODES

YARDS	T177	T178	T179	T180	T181	T182	T183	T184
0.25	4	4	2	2	2	2	2	2
0.50	10*	10*	4	4	4	4	4	4
0.75	16	16	10*	10*	10*	10*	10*	10*
1.00	20	20	10	10	10	10	10	10
1.25	28	28	20*	20*	20*	20*	14	14
1.50	32	32	20*	20*	20*	20*	20*	20*
1.75	40	40	30*	30*	30*	20	20	20
2.00	44	44	30*	30*	30*	30*	30*	22
2.25	52	52	40*	40*	30*	30*	30*	30*
2.50	56	56	40*	40*	40*	40*	30*	30*
2.75	60	60	50*	50*	40*	40*	40*	40*
3.00	68	68	50*	50*	50*	40*	40*	40*
3.25	72	72	60*	50*	50*	50*	50*	40*
3.50	80	80	60*	60*	60*	50*	50*	50*
3.75	84	84	70*	60*	60*	60*	50*	50*
4.00	92	92	70*	70*	60*	60*	60*	50*
4.25	96	96	80*	70*	70*	60*	60*	60*
4.50	104	104	80*	80*	70*	70*	60*	60*
4.75	108	108	90*	80*	80*	70*	70*	60*
5.00	112	112	90*	90*	80*	80*	70*	70*

45 " WIDE FABRIC

TEMPLATE CODES

YARDS	T177	T178	T179	T180	T181	T182	T183	T184
0.25	4	4	4	4	4	4	2	2
0.50	14*	14*	8	8	8	8	4	4
0.75	16	16	16	16	16	16	14*	14*
1.00	28*	28*	20	20	20	20	14*	14*
1.25	28	28	28	28	28	28	14	14
1.50	42*	42*	32	32	32	32	28*	28*
1.75	42*	42*	42*	42*	42*	40	28*	28*
2.00	56*	56*	44	44	44	44	42*	28*
2.25	70*	56*	56*	56*	52	52	42*	42*
2.50	70*	70*	56	56	56	56	42*	42*
2.75	84*	70*	70*	70*	64	64	56*	56*
3.00	84*	84*	70*	70*	70*	68	56*	56*
3.25	98*	84*	84*	72	72	76	70*	56*
3.50	98*	98*	84*	84*	84*	80	70*	70*
3.75	112*	98*	98*	84	84	84	70*	70*
4.00	112*	112*	98*	98*	92	92	84*	70*
4.25	126*	112*	112*	98*	98*	96	84*	84*
4.50	140*	126*	112*	112*	104	104	84*	84*
4.75	140*	126*	126*	112*	112*	108	98*	84*
5.00	154*	140*	126*	126*	116	116	98*	98*

36 " WIDE FABRIC

TEMPLATE CODES

YARDS	T185	T186	T187	T188	T189	T190	T191	T192
0.25	2	2	2	2	2	6	6	6
0.50	4	4	4	4	4	12	12	12
0.75	10*	10*	8	8	8	20*	20*	20*
1.00	10	10	10	10	10	30	30	30
1.25	14	14	14	14	14	40*	40*	36
1.50	20*	20*	16	16	16	50*	50*	42
1.75	20	20	20	20	20	60*	54	54
2.00	22	22	22	22	22	70*	60	60
2.25	30*	30*	26	26	26	80*	70*	66
2.50	30*	30*	30*	30*	28	90*	80*	78
2.75	32	32	32	32	32	100*	90*	84
3.00	40*	40*	34	34	34	110*	100*	90
3.25	40*	40*	40*	38	38	120*	100*	102
3.50	40	40	40	40	40	130*	110*	108
3.75	50*	50*	44	44	44	140*	120*	114
4.00	50*	50*	50*	46	46	150*	130*	120
4.25	50*	50*	50*	50	50	160*	140*	132
4.50	60*	60*	52	52	52	170*	150*	138
4.75	60*	60*	60*	54	54	170*	150*	144
5.00	60*	60*	60*	60*	58	180*	160*	156

45 " WIDE FABRIC

TEMPLATE CODES

YARDS	T185	T186	T187	T188	T189	T190	T191	T192
0.25	2	2	2	2	2	8	8	6
0.50	4	4	4	4	4	16	16	12
0.75	14*	14*	8	8	8	24	24	24*
1.00	14*	14*	14*	14*	14*	40	40	36*
1.25	14	14	14	14	14	48	48	36
1.50	28*	28*	16	16	16	60*	60*	48*
1.75	28*	28*	28*	28*	28*	72	72	60*
2.00	28*	28*	28*	28*	28*	84*	80	72*
2.25	42*	42*	28*	28*	28*	96*	88	72*
2.50	42*	42*	42*	42*	28	108*	104	84*
2.75	42*	42*	42*	42*	42*	120*	112	96*
3.00	56*	56*	42*	42*	42*	132*	120	108*
3.25	56*	56*	56*	42*	42*	144*	128	108*
3.50	56*	56*	56*	56*	56*	156*	144	120*
3.75	70*	70*	56*	56*	56*	168*	152	132*
4.00	70*	70*	70*	56*	56*	180*	160	144*
4.25	70*	70*	70*	70*	70*	192*	176	144*
4.50	84*	84*	70*	70*	70*	204*	184	156*
4.75	84*	84*	84*	70*	70*	204*	192	168*
5.00	84*	84*	84*	84*	70*	216*	208	180*

36 " WIDE FABRIC

TEMPLATE CODES

YARDS	T193	T194	T195	T196	T197	T198	T199	T200
0.25	4	4	4	4	4	2	2	2
0.50	10*	10*	10*	10*	10*	4	4	4
0.75	20*	12	12	16	16	10*	10*	10*
1.00	20	20	20	20	20	10	10	10
1.25	30*	30*	24	24	24	20*	20*	20*
1.50	40*	30*	30*	32	32	20*	20*	20*
1.75	40*	40*	40*	36	36	30*	30*	20*
2.00	50*	50*	40	40	40	30*	30*	30*
2.25	60*	50*	50*	48	48	40*	40*	30*
2.50	60*	60*	52	52	52	40*	40*	40*
2.75	70*	60*	60*	56	56	50*	40*	40*
3.00	80*	70*	70*	64	64	50*	50*	50*
3.25	80*	80*	70*	70*	68	60*	50*	50*
3.50	90*	80*	80*	72	72	60*	60*	50*
3.75	100*	90*	80*	80	80	70*	60*	60*
4.00	110*	100*	90*	84	84	70*	70*	60*
4.25	110*	100*	90*	90*	88	80*	70*	70*
4.50	120*	110*	100*	96	96	80*	80*	70*
4.75	130*	120*	110*	100	100	90*	80*	80*
5.00	130*	120*	110*	104	104	90*	80*	80*

45 " WIDE FABRIC

TEMPLATE CODES

YARDS	T193	T194	T195	T196	T197	T198	T199	T200
0.25	6	6	4	4	4	4	4	4
0.50	12	12	12*	12*	12*	8	8	8
0.75	24*	18	12	16	16	16	16	16
1.00	30	30	24*	24*	24*	20	20	20
1.25	36	36	24	24	24	24	24	24
1.50	48*	42	36*	36*	36*	32	32	32
1.75	54	54	48*	36	36	36	36	36
2.00	60	60	48*	48*	48*	40	40	40
2.25	72*	66	60*	48	48	48	48	48
2.50	78	78	60*	60*	60*	52	52	52
2.75	84	84	72*	60*	60*	60*	56	56
3.00	96*	90	84*	72*	72*	64	64	64
3.25	102	102	84*	84*	72*	72*	68	68
3.50	108	108	96*	84*	84*	72	72	72
3.75	120*	114	96*	96*	84*	84*	80	80
4.00	132*	126	108*	96*	96*	84	84	84
4.25	132	132	108*	108*	96*	96*	88	88
4.50	144*	138	120*	108*	108*	96	96	96
4.75	156*	150	132*	120*	108*	108*	100	100
5.00	156	156	132*	120*	120*	108*	104	104

36 " WIDE FABRIC

TEMPLATE CODES

YARDS	T201	T202	T203	T204	T205	T206	T207	T208
0.25	2	2	2	2	2	2	2	6
0.50	4	4	4	4	4	4	4	12
0.75	10*	10*	10*	10*	8	8	8	18
1.00	10	10	10	10	10	10	10	24
1.25	20*	12	12	12	12	12	12	36
1.50	20*	20*	20*	20*	16	16	16	42
1.75	20*	20*	20*	20*	20*	20*	20*	48
2.00	30*	30*	20	20	20	20	20	56*
2.25	30*	30*	30*	30*	24	24	24	64*
2.50	40*	30*	30*	30*	30*	30*	30*	72
2.75	40*	40*	30*	30*	30*	30*	30*	78
3.00	40*	40*	40*	40*	32	32	32	84
3.25	50*	40*	40*	40*	40*	40*	34	90
3.50	50*	50*	50*	40*	40*	40*	40*	96
3.75	60*	50*	50*	50*	40	40	40	108
4.00	60*	60*	50*	50*	50*	50*	42	114
4.25	60*	60*	60*	50*	50*	50*	50*	120
4.50	70*	60*	60*	60*	50*	50*	50*	128*
4.75	70*	70*	60*	60*	60*	60*	50	136*
5.00	80*	70*	70*	60*	60*	60*	60*	144

45 " WIDE FABRIC

TEMPLATE CODES

YARDS	T201	T202	T203	T204	T205	T206	T207	T208
0.25	4	2	2	2	2	2	2	8
0.50	8	4	4	4	4	4	4	16
0.75	16	12*	12*	12*	8	8	8	24
1.00	20	12*	12*	12*	12*	12*	12*	36*
1.25	24	12	12	12	12	12	12	48
1.50	32	24*	24*	24*	16	16	16	60*
1.75	36	24*	24*	24*	24*	24*	24*	72*
2.00	40	36*	24*	24*	24*	24*	24*	84*
2.25	48	36*	36*	36*	24	24	24	96*
2.50	52	36*	36*	36*	36*	36*	36*	108*
2.75	56	48*	36*	36*	36*	36*	36*	108*
3.00	64	48*	48*	48*	36*	36*	36*	120*
3.25	68	48*	48*	48*	48*	48*	36*	132*
3.50	72	60*	60*	48*	48*	48*	48*	144*
3.75	80	60*	60*	60*	48*	48*	48*	156*
4.00	84	72*	60*	60*	60*	60*	48*	168*
4.25	88	72*	72*	60*	60*	60*	60*	180*
4.50	96	72*	72*	72*	60*	60*	60*	192*
4.75	100	84*	72*	72*	72*	72*	60*	204*
5.00	104	84*	84*	72*	72*	72*	72*	216*

36 " WIDE FABRIC

TEMPLATE CODES

YARDS	T209	T210	211	T212	T213	T214	T215	T216
0.25	6	4	4	4	4	4	2	2
0.50	12	8	8	8	8	8	4	4
0.75	18	16*	16*	16*	12	12	8*	8*
1.00	24	16	16	16	16	16	8	8
1.25	36	24	24	24	24	24	16*	16*
1.50	42	32*	32*	32*	28	28	16*	16*
1.75	48	40*	32	32	32	32	24*	24*
2.00	54	40*	40*	40*	36	36	24*	24*
2.25	60	48*	48*	48*	44	44	32*	32*
2.50	72	56*	48	48	48	48	32*	32*
2.75	78	64*	56*	56*	52	52	40*	40*
3.00	84	64*	64*	64*	56	56	40*	40*
3.25	90	72*	64*	64*	64	64	48*	48*
3.50	96	80*	72*	72*	68	68	48*	48*
3.75	108	80*	80*	80*	72	72	56*	56*
4.00	114	88*	80*	80*	76	76	56*	56*
4.25	120	96*	88*	88*	84	84	64*	56*
4.50	126	104*	96*	96*	88	88	64*	64*
4.75	138	104*	96*	96*	92	92	72*	64*
5.00	144	112*	104*	104*	96	96	72*	72*

45 " WIDE FABRIC

TEMPLATE CODES

YARDS	T209	T210	211	T212	T213	T214	T215	T216
0.25	8	6	6	6	4	4	4	4
0.50	16	12	12	12	12*	12*	8	8
0.75	24	24*	24*	24*	12	12	12	12
1.00	36*	24	24	24	24*	24*	16	16
1.25	48	36	36	36	24	24	24	24
1.50	56	48*	48*	48*	36*	36*	28	28
1.75	64	60*	48	48	36*	36*	36*	36*
2.00	72	60*	60*	60*	48*	48*	36	36
2.25	84*	72*	72*	72*	60*	48*	48*	48*
2.50	96	84*	72	72	60*	60*	48	48
2.75	104	96*	84*	84*	72*	60*	60*	60*
3.00	112	96*	96*	96*	72*	72*	60*	60*
3.25	120	108*	96*	96*	84*	72*	72*	72*
3.50	132*	120*	108*	108*	84*	84*	72*	72*
3.75	144	120*	120*	120*	96*	84*	84*	84*
4.00	152	132*	120*	120*	108*	96*	84*	84*
4.25	160	144*	132*	132*	108*	108*	96*	84
4.50	168	156*	144*	144*	120*	108*	96*	96*
4.75	184	156*	144*	144*	120*	120*	108*	96*
5.00	192	168*	156*	156*	132*	120*	108*	108*

36 " WIDE FABRIC

TEMPLATE CODES

YARDS	T217	T218	T219	T220	T221	T222	T223	T224
0.25	2	2	2	2	2	2	2	2
0.50	4	4	4	4	4	4	4	4
0.75	8*	10*	10*	10*	10*	10*	6	6
1.00	8	10	10	10	10	10	10	10
1.25	16*	20*	12	12	12	12	12	12
1.50	16*	20*	20*	20*	20*	20*	14	14
1.75	24*	20*	20*	20*	20*	20*	20*	20*
2.00	24*	30*	30*	30*	20	20	20	20
2.25	24*	30*	30*	30*	30*	30*	22	22
2.50	32*	40*	30*	30*	30*	30*	30*	30*
2.75	32*	40*	40*	40*	30*	30*	30*	30*
3.00	40*	50*	40*	40*	40*	40*	30	30
3.25	40*	50*	50*	40*	40*	40*	40*	40*
3.50	48*	50*	50*	50*	50*	40*	40*	40*
3.75	48*	60*	50*	50*	50*	50*	40*	40*
4.00	56*	60*	60*	60*	50*	50*	50*	50*
4.25	56*	70*	60*	60*	60*	50*	50*	50*
4.50	56*	70*	70*	60*	60*	60*	50*	50*
4.75	64*	70*	70*	70*	60*	60*	60*	50*
5.00	64*	80*	70*	70*	70*	60*	60*	60*

45 " WIDE FABRIC

TEMPLATE CODES

YARDS	T217	T218	T219	T220	T221	T222	T223	T224
0.25	4	4	2	2	2	2	2	2
0.50	8	8	4	4	4	4	4	4
0.75	12	12	12*	12*	12*	12*	6	6
1.00	16	20	12*	12*	12*	12*	12*	12*
1.25	24	24	12	12	12	12	12	12
1.50	28	28	24*	24*	24*	24*	14	14
1.75	36*	32	24*	24*	24*	24*	24*	24*
2.00	36	40	36*	36*	24*	24*	24*	24*
2.25	44	44	36*	36*	36*	36*	24*	24*
2.50	48	48	36*	36*	36*	36*	36*	36*
2.75	52	52	48*	48*	36*	36*	36*	36*
3.00	60*	60	48*	48*	48*	48*	36*	36*
3.25	64	64	60*	48*	48*	48*	48*	48*
3.50	72*	68	60*	60*	60*	48*	48*	48*
3.75	72	72	60*	60*	60*	60*	48*	48*
4.00	84*	80	72*	72*	60*	60*	60*	60*
4.25	84	84	72*	72*	72*	60*	60*	60*
4.50	88	88	84*	72*	72*	72*	60*	60*
4.75	96*	92	84*	84*	72*	72*	72*	60*
5.00	96	100	84*	84*	84*	72*	72*	72*

36 " WIDE FABRIC

TEMPLATE CODES

YARDS	T225	T226	T227	T228	T229	T230	T231	T232
0.25	2	6	6	4	4	4	4	4
0.50	4	12	12	8	8	8	8	8
0.75	6	18	18	16*	12	12	12	12
1.00	10	24	24	16	16	16	16	16
1.25	12	32*	30	24*	24*	20	20	20
1.50	14	40*	36	32*	24	24	24	24
1.75	20*	48*	42	32*	32	32	32	32
2.00	20	48	54	40*	40*	36	36	36
2.25	22	60	60	48*	40	40	40	40
2.50	30*	66	66	56*	48*	44	44	44
2.75	30*	72	72	56*	56*	48	48	48
3.00	30	80*	78	64*	56*	56*	52	52
3.25	32	88*	84	72*	64*	56	60	60
3.50	40*	96*	90	72*	72*	64	64	64
3.75	40*	96	96	80*	72*	68	68	68
4.00	40	104*	108	88*	80*	72	72	72
4.25	50*	114	114	88*	88*	80*	76	76
4.50	50*	120	120	96*	88*	80	80	80
4.75	50*	128*	126	104*	96*	88*	84	88
5.00	60*	136*	132	112*	96*	92	92	92

45 " WIDE FABRIC

TEMPLATE CODES

YARDS	T225	T226	T227	T228	T229	T230	T231	T232
0.25	2	8	6	6	6	4	4	4
0.50	4	16	12	12	12	10*	10*	10*
0.75	6	24	20*	20*	18	12	12	12
1.00	12*	32	30*	24	24	20*	20*	20*
1.25	12	40	30	30	30	20	20	20
1.50	14	50*	40*	40*	36	30*	30*	30*
1.75	24*	60*	50*	42	48	40*	32	32
2.00	24*	64	60*	54	54	40*	40*	40*
2.25	24*	80	60	60	60	50*	50*	40
2.50	36*	88	70*	70*	66	50*	50*	50*
2.75	36*	96	80*	72	72	60*	60*	50*
3.00	36*	104	90*	80*	78	70*	60*	60*
3.25	36*	112	100*	90*	84	70*	70*	60
3.50	48*	120	100*	90	96	80*	70*	70*
3.75	48*	128	110*	102	102	80*	80*	70*
4.00	48*	136	120*	110*	108	90*	80*	80*
4.25	60*	152	130*	114	114	100*	90*	80*
4.50	60*	160	130*	120	120	100*	100*	90*
4.75	60*	168	140*	130*	126	110*	100*	90*
5.00	72*	176	150*	140*	132	110*	110*	100*

36 " WIDE FABRIC

TEMPLATE CODES

YARDS	T233	T234	T235	T236	T237	T238	T239	T240
0.25	2	2	2	2	2	2	2	2
0.50	4	4	4	4	4	4	4	4
0.75	8✱	8✱	8✱	8✱	8✱	8✱	8✱	8✱
1.00	8	8	8	8	8	8	8	8
1.25	16✱	16✱	16✱	16✱	10	10	10	10
1.50	16✱	16✱	16✱	16✱	16✱	16✱	16✱	16✱
1.75	24✱	24✱	24✱	16	16	16	16	16
2.00	24✱	24✱	24✱	24✱	24✱	18	18	18
2.25	32✱	32✱	24✱	24✱	24✱	24✱	24✱	24✱
2.50	32✱	32✱	32✱	32✱	24✱	24✱	24✱	24✱
2.75	40✱	40✱	32✱	32✱	32✱	32✱	24	24
3.00	40✱	40✱	40✱	32✱	32✱	32✱	32✱	32✱
3.25	48✱	40✱	40✱	40✱	40✱	32✱	32✱	32✱
3.50	48✱	48✱	48✱	40✱	40✱	40✱	32	32
3.75	56✱	48✱	48✱	48✱	40✱	40✱	40✱	40✱
4.00	56✱	56✱	48✱	48✱	48✱	40✱	40✱	40✱
4.25	64✱	56✱	56✱	48✱	48✱	48✱	48✱	40✱
4.50	64✱	64✱	56✱	56✱	56✱	48✱	48✱	48✱
4.75	72✱	64✱	64✱	56✱	56✱	56✱	48✱	48✱
5.00	72✱	72✱	64✱	64✱	56✱	56✱	56✱	48✱

45 " WIDE FABRIC

TEMPLATE CODES

YARDS	T233	T234	T235	T236	T237	T238	T239	T240
0.25	4	4	4	4	2	2	2	2
0.50	8	8	8	8	4	4	4	4
0.75	12	12	12	12	10✱	10✱	10✱	10✱
1.00	16	16	16	16	10✱	10✱	10✱	10✱
1.25	20	20	20	20	10	10	10	10
1.50	24	24	24	28	20✱	20✱	20✱	20✱
1.75	32	32	32	32	20✱	20✱	20✱	20✱
2.00	36	36	36	36	30✱	20✱	20✱	20✱
2.25	40	40	40	40	30✱	30✱	30✱	30✱
2.50	44	44	44	44	30✱	30✱	30✱	30✱
2.75	50✱	50✱	48	48	40✱	40✱	30✱	30✱
3.00	52	52	52	56	40✱	40✱	40✱	40✱
3.25	60	60	60	60	50✱	40✱	40✱	40✱
3.50	64	64	64	64	50✱	50✱	40✱	40✱
3.75	70✱	68	68	68	50✱	50✱	50✱	50✱
4.00	72	72	72	72	60✱	50✱	50✱	50✱
4.25	80✱	76	76	76	60✱	60✱	60✱	50✱
4.50	80	80	80	84	70✱	60✱	60✱	60✱
4.75	90✱	88	88	88	70✱	70✱	60✱	60✱
5.00	92	92	92	92	70✱	70✱	70✱	60✱

36 " WIDE FABRIC

TEMPLATE CODES

YARDS	T241	T242	T243	T244	T245	T246	T247	T248
0.25	2	2	6	4	4	4	4	4
0.50	4	4	12	8	8	8	8	8
0.75	6	6	18	16*	16*	12	12	12
1.00	8	8	24	16	16	16	16	16
1.25	10	10	32*	24*	24*	24*	20	20
1.50	14	14	36	32*	32*	24	24	24
1.75	16	16	42	40*	32*	32*	32*	28
2.00	18	18	48	40*	40*	40*	32	32
2.25	20	20	56*	48*	48*	40*	40*	36
2.50	24*	24*	64*	56*	48*	48*	40	40
2.75	24	24	72*	64*	56*	48*	48*	44
3.00	28	28	72	64*	64*	56*	48	48
3.25	32*	32*	80*	72*	64*	64*	56	56
3.50	32	32	88*	80*	72*	64*	64*	60
3.75	34	34	96*	88*	80*	72*	64	64
4.00	40*	36	104*	88*	80*	80*	72*	68
4.25	40*	40	104*	96*	88*	80*	72	72
4.50	42	42	114	104*	96*	88*	80*	76
4.75	48*	44	120	112*	96*	88*	88*	80
5.00	48*	48*	128*	112*	104*	96*	88*	84

45 " WIDE FABRIC

TEMPLATE CODES

YARDS	T241	T242	T243	T244	T245	T246	T247	T248
0.25	2	2	8	6	6	6	4	4
0.50	4	4	16	12	12	12	10*	10*
0.75	6	6	24	20*	20*	18	12	12
1.00	10*	10*	32	24	24	24	20*	20*
1.25	10	10	40	30	30	30	20	20
1.50	14	14	48	40*	40*	36	30*	30*
1.75	20*	20*	56	50*	42	42	40*	30*
2.00	20*	20*	64	50*	50*	50*	40*	40*
2.25	20	20	72	60*	60*	54	50*	40*
2.50	30*	30*	80	70*	60	60	50*	50*
2.75	30*	30*	90*	80*	70*	66	60*	50*
3.00	30*	30*	96	80*	80*	72	60*	60*
3.25	40*	40*	104	90*	80*	80*	70*	70*
3.50	40*	40*	112	100*	90*	90	80*	70*
3.75	40*	40*	120	110*	100*	96	80*	80*
4.00	50*	40*	130*	110*	102	102	90*	80*
4.25	50*	50*	136	120*	110*	108	90*	90*
4.50	50*	50*	152	130*	120*	114	100*	90*
4.75	60*	50*	160	140*	120	120	110*	100*
5.00	60*	60*	168	140*	130*	126	110*	100*

36 " WIDE FABRIC

TEMPLATE CODES

YARDS	T249	T250	T251	T252	T253	T254	T255	T256
0.25	4	2	2	2	2	2	2	2
0.50	8	4	4	4	4	4	4	4
0.75	12	8✳	8✳	8✳	8✳	8✳	8✳	8✳
1.00	16	8	8	8	8	8	8	8
1.25	20	16✳	16✳	16✳	16✳	10	10	10
1.50	24	16✳	16✳	16✳	16✳	16✳	16✳	16✳
1.75	28	24✳	24✳	16✳	16✳	16✳	16✳	16✳
2.00	32	24✳	24✳	24✳	24✳	24✳	16	16
2.25	36	32✳	32✳	24✳	24✳	24✳	24✳	24✳
2.50	40	32✳	32✳	32✳	32✳	24✳	24✳	24✳
2.75	44	40✳	32✳	32✳	32✳	32✳	32✳	24
3.00	52	40✳	40✳	40✳	32✳	32✳	32✳	32✳
3.25	56	48✳	40✳	40✳	40✳	32✳	32✳	32✳
3.50	60	48✳	48✳	40✳	40✳	40✳	40✳	32✳
3.75	64	56✳	48✳	48✳	48✳	40✳	40✳	40✳
4.00	68	56✳	56✳	48✳	48✳	48✳	40✳	40✳
4.25	72	64✳	56✳	56✳	48✳	48✳	48✳	40✳
4.50	76	64✳	64✳	56✳	56✳	48✳	48✳	48✳
4.75	80	72✳	64✳	64✳	56✳	56✳	48✳	48✳
5.00	84	72✳	64✳	64✳	64✳	56✳	56✳	48✳

45 " WIDE FABRIC

TEMPLATE CODES

YARDS	T249	T250	T251	T252	T253	T254	T255	T256
0.25	4	4	4	4	4	2	2	2
0.50	10✳	8	8	8	8	4	4	4
0.75	12	12	12	12	12	10✳	10✳	10✳
1.00	20✳	16	16	16	16	10✳	10✳	10✳
1.25	20	20	20	20	20	10	10	10
1.50	30✳	24	24	24	24	20✳	20✳	20✳
1.75	30✳	30✳	30✳	28	28	20✳	20✳	20✳
2.00	40✳	32	32	32	32	30✳	20✳	20✳
2.25	40✳	40✳	40✳	36	36	30✳	30✳	30✳
2.50	50✳	40	40	40	40	30✳	30✳	30✳
2.75	50✳	50✳	48	48	48	40✳	40✳	30✳
3.00	60✳	52	52	52	52	40✳	40✳	40✳
3.25	60✳	60✳	56	56	56	40✳	40✳	40✳
3.50	70✳	60	60	60	60	50✳	50✳	40✳
3.75	70✳	70✳	64	64	64	50✳	50✳	50✳
4.00	80✳	70✳	70✳	68	68	60✳	50✳	50✳
4.25	80✳	80✳	72	72	72	60✳	60✳	50✳
4.50	90✳	80✳	80✳	76	76	60✳	60✳	60✳
4.75	90✳	90✳	80	80	80	70✳	60✳	60✳
5.00	100✳	90✳	84	84	84	70✳	70✳	60✳

36 " WIDE FABRIC

TEMPLATE CODES

YARDS	T257	T258	T259	T260	T261	T262	T263	T264
0.25	2	2	2	0	4	4	4	4
0.50	4	4	4	6	8	8	8	8
0.75	8*	6	6	12	16*	12	12	12
1.00	8	8	8	18	16	16	16	16
1.25	10	10	10	24	24*	24*	24*	20
1.50	16*	12	12	30	32*	24	24	24
1.75	16*	16*	16*	36	40*	32*	32*	28
2.00	16	16	16	42	40*	40*	32	32
2.25	24*	18	18	48	48*	40*	40*	40*
2.50	24*	24*	24*	54	56*	48*	48*	40
2.75	24	24	24	60	56*	56*	48*	48*
3.00	32*	26	26	66	64*	56*	56*	48
3.25	32*	32*	32*	72	72*	64*	56*	56*
3.50	32*	32*	32*	78	80*	72*	64*	56
3.75	40*	32	32	84	80*	72*	72*	64*
4.00	40*	40*	34	90	88*	80*	72*	72*
4.25	40*	40*	40*	96	96*	88*	80*	72*
4.50	48*	40*	40*	102	96*	88*	80*	80*
4.75	48*	48*	40	108	104*	96*	88*	80*
5.00	48*	48*	48*	114	112*	104*	96*	88*

45 " WIDE FABRIC

TEMPLATE CODES

YARDS	T257	T258	T259	T260	T261	T262	T263	T264
0.25	2	2	2	0	6	6	6	4
0.50	4	4	4	8*	12	12	12	10*
0.75	10*	6	6	16*	20*	18	18	12
1.00	10*	10*	10*	24*	24	24	24	20*
1.25	10	10	10	24	30	30	30	20
1.50	20*	12	12	32*	40*	36	36	30*
1.75	20*	20*	20*	40*	50*	42	42	30*
2.00	20*	20*	20*	48*	50*	50*	48	40*
2.25	30*	20*	20*	56*	60*	54	54	50*
2.50	30*	30*	30*	56*	70*	60	60	50*
2.75	30*	30*	30*	64*	70*	70*	66	60*
3.00	40*	30*	30*	72*	80*	72	72	60*
3.25	40*	40*	40*	80*	90*	80*	78	70*
3.50	40*	40*	40*	88*	100*	90*	84	70*
3.75	50*	40*	40*	88*	100*	90	90	80*
4.00	50*	50*	40*	96*	110*	100*	96	90*
4.25	50*	50*	50*	104*	120*	110*	102	90*
4.50	60*	50*	50*	112*	120*	110*	108	100*
4.75	60*	60*	50*	112*	130*	120*	114	100*
5.00	60*	60*	60*	120*	140*	130*	120	110*

36 " WIDE FABRIC

TEMPLATE CODES

YARDS	T265	T266	T267	T268	T269	T270	T271	T272
0.25	4	2	2	2	2	2	2	2
0.50	8	4	4	4	4	4	4	4
0.75	12	8*	8*	8*	8*	8*	8*	8*
1.00	16	8	8	8	8	8	8	8
1.25	20	16*	16*	16*	16*	10	10	10
1.50	24	16*	16*	16*	16*	16*	16*	16*
1.75	28	24*	24*	24*	16*	16*	16*	16*
2.00	32	24*	24*	24*	24*	24*	24*	16
2.25	36	32*	32*	24*	24*	24*	24*	24*
2.50	40	32*	32*	32*	32*	24*	24*	24*
2.75	44	40*	40*	32*	32*	32*	32*	24*
3.00	48	40*	40*	40*	40*	32*	32*	32*
3.25	52	48*	48*	40*	40*	40*	32*	32*
3.50	56	48*	48*	48*	40*	40*	40*	40*
3.75	60	56*	48*	48*	48*	40*	40*	40*
4.00	64	56*	56*	56*	48*	48*	48*	40*
4.25	68	64*	56*	56*	56*	48*	48*	48*
4.50	72	64*	64*	56*	56*	56*	48*	48*
4.75	80*	72*	64*	64*	56*	56*	56*	48*
5.00	80	72*	72*	64*	64*	56*	56*	56*

45 " WIDE FABRIC

TEMPLATE CODES

YARDS	T265	T266	T267	T268	T269	T270	T271	T272
0.25	4	4	4	4	4	2	2	2
0.50	10*	8	8	8	8	4	4	4
0.75	12	12	12	12	12	10*	10*	10*
1.00	20*	16	16	16	16	10*	10*	10*
1.25	20	20	20	20	20	10	10	10
1.50	30*	24	24	24	24	20*	20*	20*
1.75	30*	30*	30*	30*	28	20*	20*	20*
2.00	40*	32	32	32	32	30*	30*	20*
2.25	40*	40*	40*	36	36	30*	30*	30*
2.50	50*	40	40	40	40	30*	30*	30*
2.75	50*	50*	50*	44	44	40*	40*	30*
3.00	60*	50*	50*	50*	50*	40*	40*	40*
3.25	60*	60*	60*	52	52	50*	40*	40*
3.50	70*	60*	60*	60*	56	50*	50*	50*
3.75	70*	70*	60	60	60	50*	50*	50*
4.00	80*	70*	70*	70*	64	60*	60*	50*
4.25	80*	80*	70*	70*	70*	60*	60*	60*
4.50	90*	80*	80*	72	72	70*	60*	60*
4.75	100*	90*	80*	80*	76	70*	70*	60*
5.00	100*	90*	90*	80	80	70*	70*	70*

36 " WIDE FABRIC

TEMPLATE CODES

YARDS	T273	T274	T275	T276	T277	T278	T279	T280
0.25	2	2	2	0	0	0	0	0
0.50	4	4	4	6	6*	6*	6*	6*
0.75	8*	6	6	12	12*	8	8	8
1.00	8	8	8	18	12	12	12	12
1.25	10	10	10	24	18*	18*	16	16
1.50	16*	12	12	30	24*	20	20	20
1.75	16*	16*	16*	36	24	24	24	24
2.00	16	16	16	42	30*	30*	28	28
2.25	24*	18	18	48	36*	32	32	32
2.50	24*	24*	24*	54	36	36	36	36
2.75	24*	24*	24*	60	42*	40	40	40
3.00	32*	24	24	66	48*	44	44	44
3.25	32*	32*	32*	72	48	48	48	48
3.50	32*	32*	32*	78	54*	52	52	52
3.75	40*	32*	32*	84	60*	56	56	56
4.00	40*	40*	40*	90	66*	60	60	60
4.25	40*	40*	40*	96	66*	64	64	64
4.50	48*	40*	40*	96	72*	68	68	68
4.75	48*	48*	48*	102	78*	72	72	72
5.00	48*	48*	48*	108	78*	76	76	76

45 " WIDE FABRIC

TEMPLATE CODES

YARDS	T273	T274	T275	T276	T277	T278	T279	T280
0.25	2	2	2	0	0	0	0	0
0.50	4	4	4	8*	8*	8*	8*	8*
0.75	10*	6	6	16*	16*	12	8	8
1.00	10*	10*	10*	24	18	18	16*	16*
1.25	10	10	10	24	24	24	16	16
1.50	20*	12	12	32*	32*	30	24*	24*
1.75	20*	20*	20*	40*	36	36	32*	24
2.00	20*	20*	20*	48*	42	42	32*	32*
2.25	30*	20*	20*	48	48	48	40*	32
2.50	30*	30*	30*	56*	54	54	40*	40*
2.75	30*	30*	30*	64*	60	60	48*	48*
3.00	40*	30*	30*	72*	66	66	56*	48*
3.25	40*	40*	40*	72	72	72	56*	56*
3.50	40*	40*	40*	80*	78	78	64*	56*
3.75	50*	40*	40*	88*	84	84	64*	64*
4.00	50*	50*	50*	96*	90	90	72*	64*
4.25	50*	50*	50*	96	96	96	80*	72*
4.50	60*	50*	50*	104*	102	102	80*	72*
4.75	60*	60*	60*	112*	108	108	88*	80*
5.00	60*	60*	60*	120*	108	114	88*	80*

36 " WIDE FABRIC

TEMPLATE CODES

YARDS	T281	T282	T283	T284	T285	T286	T287	T288
0.25	0	0	0	0	0	0	0	0
0.50	6*	2	2	2	2	2	2	2
0.75	8	6*	6*	6*	6*	6*	6*	6*
1.00	12	6	6	6	6	6	6	6
1.25	16	12*	12*	12*	12*	8	8	8
1.50	20	12*	12*	12*	12*	12*	12*	12*
1.75	24	18*	18*	18*	12	12	12	12
2.00	28	18*	18*	18*	18*	18*	14	14
2.25	32	24*	24*	18*	18*	18*	18*	18*
2.50	36	24*	24*	24*	24*	18	18	18
2.75	40	30*	30*	24*	24*	24*	24*	20
3.00	44	30*	30*	30*	24*	24*	24*	24*
3.25	48	36*	30*	30*	30*	30*	24	24
3.50	52	36*	36*	36*	30*	30*	30*	26
3.75	56	42*	36*	36*	36*	30*	30*	30*
4.00	60	42*	42*	36*	36*	36*	30	30
4.25	64	48*	42*	42*	36*	36*	36*	36*
4.50	68	48*	48*	42*	42*	42*	36*	36*
4.75	72	54*	48*	48*	42*	42*	42*	36
5.00	76	54*	54*	48*	48*	42*	42*	42*

45 " WIDE FABRIC

TEMPLATE CODES

YARDS	T281	T282	T283	T284	T285	T286	T287	T288
0.25	0	0	0	0	0	0	0	0
0.50	8*	4	4	4	4	2	2	2
0.75	8	8	8	8	8	8*	8*	8*
1.00	16*	12	12	12	12	8*	8*	8*
1.25	16	16	16	16	16	8	8	8
1.50	24*	20	20	20	20	16*	16*	16*
1.75	24	24	24	24	24	16*	16*	16*
2.00	32*	28	28	28	28	24*	16*	16*
2.25	32	32	32	32	32	24*	24*	24*
2.50	40*	36	36	36	36	24*	24*	24*
2.75	40	40	40	40	40	32*	32*	24*
3.00	48*	44	44	44	44	32*	32*	32*
3.25	48	48	48	48	48	40*	32*	32*
3.50	56*	52	52	52	52	40*	40*	32*
3.75	56	56	56	56	56	40*	40*	40*
4.00	64*	60	60	60	60	48*	40*	40*
4.25	64	64	64	64	64	48*	48*	48*
4.50	72*	68	68	68	68	56*	48*	48*
4.75	72	72	72	72	72	56*	56*	48*
5.00	80*	76	76	76	76	56*	56*	56*

36 " WIDE FABRIC

TEMPLATE CODES

YARDS	T289	T290	T291	T292	T293	T294	T295	T296
0.25	0	0	0	0	0	0	0	0
0.50	2	2	2	6*	6*	6*	6*	6*
0.75	6*	4	4	12*	8	8	8	8
1.00	6	6	6	12	12	12	12	12
1.25	8	8	8	18*	18*	18*	16	16
1.50	12*	10	10	24*	20	20	20	20
1.75	12	12	12	30*	24	24	24	24
2.00	14	14	14	30*	30*	28	28	28
2.25	18*	16	16	36*	32	32	32	32
2.50	18	18	18	42*	36	36	36	36
2.75	20	20	20	42*	42*	36	36	40
3.00	24*	22	22	48*	42*	42*	40	40
3.25	24	24	24	54*	48*	48*	44	44
3.50	26	26	26	60*	54*	48	48	48
3.75	30*	28	28	60*	54*	54*	52	52
4.00	30	30	30	66*	60*	56	56	56
4.25	32	32	32	72*	66*	60	60	60
4.50	36*	34	34	78*	66*	66*	64	64
4.75	36	36	36	78*	72*	68	68	68
5.00	38	38	38	84*	78*	72	72	72

45 " WIDE FABRIC

TEMPLATE CODES

YARDS	T289	T290	T291	T292	T293	T294	T295	T296
0.25	0	0	0	0	0	0	0	0
0.50	2	2	2	8*	8*	8*	8*	8*
0.75	8*	4	4	16*	12	12	8	8
1.00	8*	8*	8*	18	18	18	16*	16*
1.25	8	8	8	24	24	24	16	16
1.50	16*	10	10	32*	30	30	24*	24*
1.75	16*	16*	16*	40*	36	36	32*	24
2.00	16*	16*	16*	42	42	42	32*	32*
2.25	24*	16	16	48	48	48	40*	32
2.50	24*	24*	24*	56*	54	54	40*	40*
2.75	24*	24*	24*	56*	56*	54	48*	40
3.00	32*	24*	24*	64*	60	60	48*	48*
3.25	32*	32*	32*	72*	66	66	56*	48*
3.50	32*	32*	32*	80*	72	72	64*	56*
3.75	40*	32*	32*	80*	78	78	64*	64*
4.00	40*	40*	40*	88*	84	84	72*	64*
4.25	40*	40*	40*	96*	90	90	72*	72*
4.50	48*	40*	40*	104*	96	96	80*	72*
4.75	48*	48*	40*	104*	102	102	80*	80*
5.00	48*	48*	48*	112*	108	108	88*	80*

36 " WIDE FABRIC

TEMPLATE CODES

YARDS	T297	T298	T299	T300	T301	T302	T303	T304
0.25	0	0	0	0	0	0	0	0
0.50	6✳	2	2	2	2	2	2	2
0.75	8	6✳	6✳	6✳	6✳	6✳	6✳	6✳
1.00	12	6	6	6	6	6	6	6
1.25	16	12✳	12✳	12✳	12✳	8	8	8
1.50	20	12✳	12✳	12✳	12✳	12✳	12✳	12✳
1.75	24	18✳	18✳	12	12	12	12	12
2.00	28	18✳	18✳	18✳	18✳	18✳	14	14
2.25	32	24✳	24✳	18✳	18✳	18✳	18✳	18✳
2.50	36	24✳	24✳	24✳	24✳	18	18	18
2.75	40	30✳	24✳	24✳	24✳	24✳	24✳	20
3.00	40	30✳	30✳	30✳	24✳	24✳	24✳	24✳
3.25	44	36✳	30✳	30✳	30✳	24	24	24
3.50	48	36✳	36✳	30✳	30✳	30✳	30✳	24
3.75	52	42✳	36✳	36✳	36✳	30✳	30✳	30✳
4.00	56	42✳	42✳	36✳	36✳	36✳	30✳	30✳
4.25	60	48✳	42✳	42✳	36✳	36✳	36✳	30
4.50	64	48✳	48✳	42✳	42✳	36✳	36✳	36✳
4.75	68	48✳	48✳	48✳	42✳	42✳	36✳	36✳
5.00	72	54✳	48✳	48✳	48✳	42✳	42✳	36

45 " WIDE FABRIC

TEMPLATE CODES

YARDS	T297	T298	T299	T300	T301	T302	T303	T304
0.25	0	0	0	0	0	0	0	0
0.50	8✳	4	4	4	4	2	2	2
0.75	8	8	8	8	8	8✳	8✳	8✳
1.00	16✳	12	12	12	12	8✳	8✳	8✳
1.25	16	16	16	16	16	8	8	8
1.50	24✳	20	20	20	20	16✳	16✳	16✳
1.75	24	24	24	24	24	16✳	16✳	16✳
2.00	32✳	28	28	28	28	24✳	16✳	16✳
2.25	32	32	32	32	32	24✳	24✳	24✳
2.50	40✳	36	36	36	36	24✳	24✳	24✳
2.75	40	40	40	40	40	32✳	32✳	24✳
3.00	48✳	40	44	44	44	32✳	32✳	32✳
3.25	48✳	48✳	44	44	44	32✳	32✳	32✳
3.50	56✳	48	48	48	48	40✳	40✳	32✳
3.75	56✳	56✳	52	52	52	40✳	40✳	40✳
4.00	64✳	56	56	56	56	48✳	40✳	40✳
4.25	64✳	64✳	60	60	60	48✳	48✳	40✳
4.50	72✳	64	64	64	64	48✳	48✳	48✳
4.75	72✳	68	68	68	68	56✳	48✳	48✳
5.00	80✳	72	72	72	72	56✳	56✳	48✳

36 " WIDE FABRIC

TEMPLATE CODES

YARDS	T305	T306	T307	T308	T309	T310	T311	T312
0.25	0	0	0	0	0	0	0	0
0.50	2	2	6*	6*	6*	6*	2	2
0.75	6*	4	8	8	8	8	6*	6*
1.00	6	6	12	12	12	12	6	6
1.25	8	8	18*	16	16	16	12*	12*
1.50	12*	10	20	20	20	20	12*	12*
1.75	12	12	24	24	24	24	18*	18*
2.00	14	14	30*	24	24	24	18*	18*
2.25	18*	16	30*	30*	28	28	24*	24*
2.50	18	18	36*	32	32	32	24*	24*
2.75	20	20	42*	36	36	36	30*	30*
3.00	24*	22	42*	42*	40	40	30*	30*
3.25	24	24	48*	44	44	44	36*	30*
3.50	24	24	54*	48	48	48	36*	36*
3.75	30*	26	54*	48	48	52	42*	36*
4.00	30*	30*	60*	54*	52	52	42*	42*
4.25	30	30	60*	60*	56	56	48*	42*
4.50	36*	32	66*	60	60	60	48*	48*
4.75	36*	36*	72*	66*	64	64	54*	48*
5.00	36	36	72*	68	68	68	54*	54*

45 " WIDE FABRIC

TEMPLATE CODES

YARDS	T305	T306	T307	T308	T309	T310	T311	T312
0.25	0	0	0	0	0	0	0	0
0.50	2	2	8*	8*	8*	8*	4	4
0.75	8*	4	12	8	8	8	8	8
1.00	8*	8*	18	16*	16*	16*	12	12
1.25	8	8	24	16	16	16	16	16
1.50	16*	10	30	24*	24*	24*	20	20
1.75	16*	16*	36	32*	24	24	24	24
2.00	16*	16*	40*	32*	32*	32*	24	24
2.25	24*	16	42	40*	32*	32*	32*	32*
2.50	24*	24*	48	40*	40*	40*	32	32
2.75	24*	24*	56*	48	48*	40*	40*	40*
3.00	32*	24*	60	56*	48*	48*	40	40
3.25	32*	32*	66	56*	56*	48*	48*	44
3.50	32*	32*	72	64*	56*	56*	48	48
3.75	40*	32*	72	64*	64*	56*	56*	52
4.00	40*	40*	80*	72*	64*	64*	56*	56*
4.25	40*	40*	· 84	80*	72*	64*	64*	56
4.50	48*	40*	90	80*	72*	72*	64*	64*
4.75	48*	48*	96	88*	80*	72*	72*	64
5.00	48*	48*	102	88*	88*	80*	72*	72*

36 " WIDE FABRIC

TEMPLATE CODES

YARDS	T313	T314	T315	T316	T317	T318	T319	T320
0.25	0	0	0	0	0	0	0	0
0.50	2	2	2	2	2	2	2	2
0.75	6*	6*	6*	6*	6*	6*	4	4
1.00	6	6	6	6	6	6	6	6
1.25	12*	12*	8	8	8	8	8	8
1.50	12*	12*	12*	12*	12*	12*	10	10
1.75	18*	12	12	12	12	12	12	12
2.00	18*	18*	18*	18*	14	14	14	14
2.25	18*	18*	18*	18*	18*	18*	14	14
2.50	24*	24*	18*	18*	18*	18*	18*	18*
2.75	24*	24*	24*	24*	18	18	18	18
3.00	30*	24*	24*	24*	24*	24*	20	20
3.25	30*	30*	30*	24*	24*	24*	24*	24*
3.50	36*	30*	30*	30*	30*	24	24	24
3.75	36*	36*	30*	30*	30*	30*	26	26
4.00	36*	36*	36*	36*	30*	30*	30*	30*
4.25	42*	42*	36*	36*	36*	30*	30*	30*
4.50	42*	42*	42*	36*	36*	36*	30	30
4.75	48*	42*	42*	42*	36*	36*	36*	36*
5.00	48*	48*	42*	42*	42*	36*	36*	36*

45 " WIDE FABRIC

TEMPLATE CODES

YARDS	T313	T314	T315	T316	T317	T318	T319	T320
0.25	0	0	0	0	0	0	0	0
0.50	4	4	2	2	2	2	2	2
0.75	8	8	8*	8*	8*	8*	4	4
1.00	12	12	8*	8*	8*	8*	8*	8*
1.25	16	16	8	8	8	8	8	8
1.50	20	20	16*	16*	16*	16*	10	10
1.75	24	24	16*	16*	16*	16*	16*	16*
2.00	24	24	24*	24*	16*	16*	16*	16*
2.25	28	28	24*	24*	24*	24*	16*	16*
2.50	32	32	24*	24*	24*	24*	24*	24*
2.75	36	36	32*	32*	24*	24*	24*	24*
3.00	40	40	32*	32*	32*	32*	24*	24*
3.25	44	44	40*	32*	32*	32*	32*	32*
3.50	48	48	40*	40*	40*	32*	32*	32*
3.75	52	52	40*	40*	40*	40*	32*	32*
4.00	52	52	48*	48*	40*	40*	40*	40*
4.25	56	56	48*	48*	48*	40*	40*	40*
4.50	60	60	56*	48*	48*	48*	40*	40*
4.75	64	64	56*	56*	48*	48*	48*	48*
5.00	68	68	56*	56*	56*	48*	48*	48*

36 " WIDE FABRIC

TEMPLATE CODES

YARDS	T321	T322	T323	T324	T325	T326	T327	T328
0.25	0	0	0	0	0	0	0	0
0.50	6*	6*	6*	6*	2	2	2	2
0.75	8	8	8	8	6*	6*	6*	6*
1.00	12	12	12	12	6	6	6	6
1.25	18*	16	16	16	12*	12*	12*	12*
1.50	18*	18*	18*	18*	12*	12*	12*	12*
1.75	24*	24*	20	20	18*	18*	12*	12*
2.00	24	24	24	24	18*	18*	18*	18*
2.25	30*	30*	28	28	24*	24*	18*	18*
2.50	36*	32	32	32	24*	24*	24*	24*
2.75	36*	36	36	36	30*	24*	24*	24*
3.00	42*	36	36	36	30*	30*	30*	24*
3.25	48*	42*	42*	40	36*	30*	30*	30*
3.50	48*	48*	44	44	36*	36*	30*	30*
3.75	54*	48	48	48	42*	36*	36*	36*
4.00	54*	54*	52	52	42*	42*	36*	36*
4.25	60*	54*	56	56	48*	42*	42*	36*
4.50	66*	60*	56	56	48*	48*	42*	42*
4.75	66*	60	60	60	54*	48*	48*	42*
5.00	72*	66*	64	64	54*	54*	48*	48*

45 " WIDE FABRIC

TEMPLATE CODES

YARDS	T321	T322	T323	T324	T325	T326	T327	T328
0.25	0	0	0	0	0	0	0	0
0.50	8*	8*	8*	8*	4	4	4	4
0.75	12	8	8	8	8	8	8	8
1.00	18	16*	16*	16*	12	12	12	12
1.25	24	16	16	16	16	16	16	16
1.50	24	24*	24*	24*	16	16	16	20
1.75	32*	32*	24*	24*	24*	24*	20	20
2.00	36	32*	32*	32*	24	24	24	24
2.25	42	40*	32*	32*	32*	32*	28	28
2.50	48	40*	40*	40*	32	32	32	32
2.75	48	48*	40*	40*	40*	36	36	36
3.00	56*	48*	48*	48*	40*	40*	40*	40
3.25	64*	56*	56*	48*	48*	40	40	40
3.50	66	64*	56*	56*	48*	48*	44	44
3.75	72	64*	64*	56*	56*	48	48	48
4.00	78	72*	64*	64*	56*	56*	52	52
4.25	80*	72*	72*	64*	64*	56	56	56
4.50	88*	80*	72*	72*	64*	64*	56	60
4.75	90	80*	80*	72*	72*	64*	64*	60
5.00	96	88*	80*	80*	72*	72*	64	64

36 " WIDE FABRIC

TEMPLATE CODES

YARDS	T329	T330	T331	T332	T333	T334	T335	T336
0.25	0	0	0	0	0	0	0	0
0.50	2	2	2	2	2	6*	6*	6*
0.75	6*	6*	6*	6*	4	8	8	8
1.00	6	6	6	6	6	12	12	12
1.25	8	8	8	8	8	18*	18*	12
1.50	12*	12*	12*	12*	10	18*	18*	18*
1.75	12*	12*	12*	12*	12*	24*	24*	20
2.00	18*	12	12	12	12	30*	24	24
2.25	18*	18*	18*	18*	14	30*	30*	30*
2.50	18*	18*	18*	18*	18*	36*	36*	30*
2.75	24*	24*	18	18	18	42*	36*	36*
3.00	24*	24*	24*	24*	20	42*	42*	36
3.25	30*	24*	24*	24*	24*	48*	42*	42*
3.50	30*	30*	24*	24*	24*	54*	48*	42*
3.75	30*	30*	30*	30*	24	54*	54*	48*
4.00	36*	30*	30*	30*	30*	60*	54*	48
4.25	36*	36*	36*	30*	30*	66*	60*	54*
4.50	36*	36*	36*	36*	30	66*	60*	60*
4.75	42*	42*	36*	36*	36*	72*	66*	60*
5.00	42*	42*	42*	36*	36*	72*	72*	66*

45 " WIDE FABRIC

TEMPLATE CODES

YARDS	T329	T330	T331	T332	T333	T334	T335	T336
0.25	0	0	0	0	0	0	0	0
0.50	2	2	2	2	2	6	6	6*
0.75	8*	8*	8*	8*	4	12	12	8
1.00	8*	8*	8*	8*	8*	18	18	12
1.25	8	8	8	8	8	18	18	12
1.50	16*	16*	16*	16*	10	24	24	18*
1.75	16*	16*	16*	16*	16*	30	30	20
2.00	24*	16*	16*	16*	16*	36	36	24
2.25	24*	24*	24*	24*	16*	42	42	30*
2.50	24*	24*	24*	24*	24*	42	42	30*
2.75	32*	32*	24*	24*	24*	48	48	36*
3.00	32*	32*	32*	32*	24*	54	54	36
3.25	40*	32*	32*	32*	32*	60	60	42*
3.50	40*	40*	32*	32*	32*	60	60	42*
3.75	40*	40*	40*	40*	32*	66	66	48*
4.00	48*	40*	40*	40*	40*	72	72	48
4.25	48*	48*	48*	40*	40*	78	78	54*
4.50	48*	48*	48*	48*	40*	84	84	60*
4.75	56*	56*	48*	48*	48*	84	84	60*
5.00	56*	56*	56*	48*	48*	90	90	66*

36 " WIDE FABRIC

TEMPLATE CODES

YARDS	T337	T338	T339	T340	T341	T342	T343	T344
0.25	0	0	0	0	0	0	0	0
0.50	6*	2	2	2	2	2	2	2
0.75	8	6*	6*	6*	6*	6*	6*	6*
1.00	12	6	6	6	6	6	6	6
1.25	12	12*	12*	12*	12*	6	6	6
1.50	18*	12*	12*	12*	12*	12*	12*	12*
1.75	20	18*	18*	18*	12*	12*	12*	12*
2.00	24	18*	18*	18*	18*	18*	18*	12
2.25	28	24*	24*	18*	18*	18*	18*	18*
2.50	30*	24*	24*	24*	24*	18*	18*	18*
2.75	32	30*	30*	24*	24*	24*	24*	18*
3.00	36	30*	30*	30*	30*	24*	24*	24*
3.25	40	36*	36*	30*	30*	30*	24*	24*
3.50	44	36*	36*	36*	30*	30*	30*	30*
3.75	44	42*	36*	36*	36*	30*	30*	30*
4.00	48	42*	42*	42*	36*	36*	36*	30*
4.25	52	48*	42*	42*	42*	36*	36*	36*
4.50	56	48*	48*	42*	42*	42*	36*	36*
4.75	56	54*	48*	48*	42*	42*	42*	36*
5.00	60	54*	54*	48*	48*	42*	42*	42*

45 " WIDE FABRIC

TEMPLATE CODES

YARDS	T337	T338	T339	T340	T341	T342	T343	T344
0.25	0	0	0	0	0	0	0	0
0.50	6*	4	4	4	4	2	2	2
0.75	8	8	8	8	8	6*	6*	6*
1.00	12	12	12	12	12	6	6	6
1.25	12	12	12	12	12	6	6	6
1.50	18*	16	16	16	16	12*	12*	12*
1.75	20	20	20	20	20	12*	12*	12*
2.00	24	24	24	24	24	18*	18*	12
2.25	28	28	28	28	28	18*	18*	18*
2.50	30*	28	28	28	28	18*	18*	18*
2.75	32	32	32	32	32	24*	24*	18*
3.00	36	36	36	36	36	24*	24*	24*
3.25	40	40	40	40	40	30*	24*	24*
3.50	44	44	44	44	44	30*	30*	30*
3.75	44	44	44	44	44	30*	30*	30*
4.00	48	48	48	48	48	36*	36*	30*
4.25	52	52	52	52	52	36*	36*	36*
4.50	56	56	56	56	56	42*	36*	36*
4.75	56	56	60	60	60	42*	42*	36*
5.00	60	60	60	60	60	42*	42*	42*

36 " WIDE FABRIC

YARDS	T345	T346	T347
0.25	0	0	0
0.50	2	2	2
0.75	6*	4	4
1.00	6	6	6
1.25	6	6	8
1.50	12*	8	8
1.75	12*	12*	12*
2.00	12	12	12
2.25	18*	14	14
2.50	18*	18*	18*
2.75	18*	18*	18*
3.00	24*	18	18
3.25	24*	24*	24*
3.50	24*	24*	24*
3.75	30*	24*	24
4.00	30*	30*	30*
4.25	30*	30*	30*
4.50	36*	30*	30*
4.75	36*	36*	36*
5.00	36*	36*	36*

45 " WIDE FABRIC

YARDS	T345	T346	T347
0.25	0	0	0
0.50	2	2	2
0.75	6*	4	4
1.00	6	6	8*
1.25	6	6	8
1.50	12*	8	8
1.75	12*	12*	16*
2.00	12	12	16*
2.25	18*	14	16*
2.50	18*	18*	24*
2.75	18*	18*	24*
3.00	24*	18	24*
3.25	24*	24*	32*
3.50	24*	24*	32*
3.75	30*	24*	32*
4.00	30*	30*	40*
4.25	30*	30*	40*
4.50	36*	30*	40*
4.75	36*	36*	48*
5.00	36*	36*	48*